The Poultry Cookbook

The Poultry Cookbook

Mary Norwak

Elm Tree Books · London

First published in Great Britain 1979
by Elm Tree Books/Hamish Hamilton Ltd
Garden House 57–59 Long Acre London WC2E 9JZ

Published in the United States of America by
Elm Tree Books in association with David & Charles Inc,
North Pomfret, Vermont 05053, USA

Book Design by Logos Design

British Library Cataloguing in Publication Data

Norwak, Mary
  The poultry cookbook.
  1. Cookery (Chicken)
  I. Title
  64.6'6'5   TX750   78–41226
  ISBN 0–241–89807–2

Typeset by Filmtype Services Ltd, Scarborough
Printed in Great Britain by
Lowe & Brydone Printers Ltd, Thetford, Norfolk

Contents

Introduction

Je veux qu'il n'y ait si pauvre paysan en mon Royaume qu'il n'ait tous les dimanches sa poule au pot (I want there to be no peasant in my Kingdom so poor that he is unable to have a chicken in his pot every Sunday).

Such were the stirring words of Henry IV in France, and what nobler aim could there be for any monarch in the days when peasant poverty meant living on little but sour-tasting bread and fat bacon. For centuries chicken was a feasting food, provided for special occasions, family reunions and Sunday meals for guests, but in recent times a revolution has taken place. Modern farming techniques have truly produced a 'chicken for every pot', and today we can pick up a chicken for any weekday supper and use portions for a single meal or for a picnic, as well as serving it for those special occasions.

Nutritionally, chicken is first-class family fare. It has one of the highest protein contents of any food, yielding 8.4 g of protein per oz against 6 g for roast beef. Those who are concerned about high cholesterol levels in the blood can be reassured about chicken, for the fat does not increase the blood cholesterol level. Weightwatchers can eat chicken with a clear conscience as a 75-g (3-oz) helping of roast chicken yields a count of only 178 calories (the same quantity of roast pork has 387!).

To me, the most important quality of a chicken is its versatility and delicious flavour when cooked in so many ways. Today, I can buy a fresh or frozen bird of any size I like, or I can buy just a few joints to suit the meal I am preparing. If I want to prepare a special dish, I can buy a pack of chicken breasts; for pâté-making or omelettes, there are boxes of livers. And as meal prices continue to rise, chicken represents really good value for money. When I have cooked a roast chicken (with all those delicious trimmings), I know I can feed the family economically on a second-day hot dish, an omelette, and some potted chicken for sandwiches, and will still have a big pot of stock for two kinds of soup. Nothing is wasted. There is also the convenience that I can freeze these additional items if I don't need them at once, and indeed I can keep a chicken and some portions always on hand for days when shopping is not convenient.

The dishes in this book demonstrate the versatility of chicken, ranging from the simple and homely to the frankly exotic, but all of them are very easy to prepare. They have been tested with birds weighing 1.35–1.5 kg (3–3½ lb) as these are most readily available from all sources. With a large family, I prefer to buy a larger bird to yield extra meals, in which case the recipes are readily adaptable as all are generous with stuffings and sauces, but do allow longer cooking time for larger birds.

The ingredients for each recipe are given in metric, with roughly equivalent imperial measures in brackets. It is important that either one set or the other is followed, as the different measures are not interchangeable and a lack of 'balance' will result.

As I am also a 'turkey fan', and as these birds are now so readily available and can often be used for chicken recipes, I have included a chapter on ways of cooking and serving turkey.

1   Choosing, Preparing and Carving a Chicken

While most of today's birds are oven-ready, neatly drawn and trussed with their accompanying giblets packaged for use, there is still a little preparation necessary in thawing the bird and getting it ready for your chosen method of cooking. A fresh bird is usually drawn and trussed by the butcher, but it is still useful to know all the stages of preparation, from killing to cooking, in case you are ever faced with a bird in its natural state. Even when the bird is bought frozen and oven-ready, you may want to joint or bone it for a special dish, and this is not difficult with the right tools. The only necessary items are a sharp knife and a pair of secateurs or poultry shears. For jointing, a heavy weight, such as a scale weight, is useful (a can of food can be used otherwise), and a trussing needle and string are necessary to finish off a bird neatly.

Choosing a chicken

Chicken can be bought in many shapes and sizes depending upon your taste and the manner in which you do your shopping – from birds drawn and trussed in the butchers' shops to a fresh-frozen, oven-ready bird from the local supermarket.

Housewives seeking extra large chickens can buy capons, although demand for these birds is apt to be very seasonal. Boiling fowl are a good buy but they should always be cooked slowly. This type of bird is older than the usual oven-ready chicken, but producers do make the distinction on the packaging by calling it 'boiling fowl', 'steam roaster' or 'slow roaster'. Chicken portions – quarters, breasts, drumsticks, wings and thighs – are sold fresh and frozen, singly or in multiple packs.

THAWING

Frozen chicken *must* be completely thawed before cooking. To obtain the best results, birds should be thawed slowly. Ideally they should be thawed in a refrigerator at a temperature of 4.4°C (40°F). Good results can also be obtained by thawing at normal kitchen temperature of around 16°C (65°F).

Weight	Thawed at room temperature 16°C (65°F)	Thawed in refrigerator 4.4°C (40°F)
kg (lb)	hrs	hrs
1 (2)	8	28
1.35 (3)	9	32
2 (4)	10	38
2.5 (5)	12	44
3 (6)	14	50
3.5 (7)	16	56

Remember that, once thawed, poultry is as perishable as any fresh meat and should be cooked as soon as possible. Do not re-freeze once thawed. Frozen poultry can be stored in the freezer for up to nine months, but should be thawed out carefully before cooking.

SIX BASIC WAYS TO COOK A CHICKEN

Method	Time	Temperature
oven-roasting	$1\frac{1}{4}$ hrs: 1.5 kg ($3\frac{1}{2}$ lb)	200°C (400°F)/Gas 7
spit-roasting	1 hr: 1.35 kg (3 lb)	medium fast
grilling	10–15 mins per side	hot – 10 cm (4 in) from heat
frying	15–20 mins per side	faintly smoking
deep-frying	approx 15 mins	faintly smoking
casseroling	30–40 mins for joints	simmering 170°C
	$1\frac{1}{2}$ hrs: 1.35 kg (3 lb)	(325°F)/Gas 4

Oven-roast Stuff the bird at the neck end. Rub skin with seasoning and butter and place in the preheated oven.

Spit-roast Do not stuff the bird but season well. Make sure it is properly trussed with string and secure on the spit. Baste constantly for an even colour.

Grill Chicken may be skinned and boned or not; but should be well seasoned and brushed with oil.

Fry (in shallow/deep fat) Chicken may be skinned and boned, or not. Dip in seasoned flour for shallow frying or coat in egg and crumbs for deep frying.

Casserole Dip chicken in seasoned flour and fry to seal and colour. Add stock and vegetables.

It is not difficult to joint a bird at home. Make sure a frozen bird is completely thawed before cutting. You need a strong sharp knife, a chopping board and a weight.

1 Before cutting remove fat from inside carcase, cut off parson's nose. Cut off end of drumsticks and ends of wings.

2 Place chicken on chopping board and, with a strong sharp knife, cut lengthwise all along the breastbone – open bird out and cut through length of backbone. Tap knife sharply with heavy weight where necessary.

3 Lay halves of chicken on board and divide each in half again by cutting diagonally between wing and thigh. The chicken is now in four quarters – two breasts and wing quarters, two thigh and drumstick quarters.

4 To make 6 portions, separate each thigh and drumstick quarter in half by cutting through at ball and socket joint. The portions can be skinned if preferred.

Plucking

It is easiest to pluck a bird when seated, with the bird's head hanging down. Have a sack or large box handy for the feathers. Beginning at the back, pick down the neck to within about 7.5 cm (3 in) of the head. Turn the bird and continue on breast, legs and wings. The skin tears very easily, and it sometimes helps to hold the flesh with the left hand while plucking with the right. Some people pluck with the growth of the feathers, which are at a slight angle to the body; others prefer to pluck in the opposite direction, but it is best to continue in one direction and not change in the middle of plucking a bird.

Drawing

Cut off the feet below the knee joint with a pair of secateurs or poultry shears. Put the bird breast downwards and pick up a fold of skin at the base of the neck. Thrust a knife through and cut towards the head, leaving a flap of skin, then pull the skin away to leave the neck exposed. Cut the neck off close to the body with secateurs, shears or a knife. Double the neck back over the head and cut the skin, making a flap. Put the fingers inside the hole below the neck and loosen the crop. Loosen the lungs and break away all internally securing membranes.

Make a hole by cutting above the vent below the parson's nose. Put a finger into the hole and pick up the intestines. Insert a knife and cut out the vent. Take hold of the vent and pull, and a length of intestine will come away with it. Press behind the gizzard and force it out. Pick up the gizzard and pull out all the organs. Flatten the wings and trim the ends. Fold the first flap of the skin over the end of the neck, and close the neck opening with the second flap. Truss the bird neatly with string.

11

Trussing

It does not take long to truss a chicken, but a trussing needle is essential. This is about 25 cm (10 in) long with an eye big enough to take fine string. The pointed end is usually flat, rather like the tip of a knife, so that it penetrates flesh easily. Nothing else will do instead, as the needle has to be long enough to go right through the bird so that both ends show at the same time.

To truss a bird, pull the front flap of skin over the neck cavity and under the bird. Twist the wing tips so that they lie neatly underneath the bird. Put a good length of string through the eye of the needle and push the needle into one wing. Catch the neck skin underneath with an in and out stitch and bring the needle out through the opposite wing. Pull the needle and string through, leaving a tail of string on one side. Push the needle back through the thickest part of the thigh and take it through the opposite thigh. Tie the loose end and the string on the needle and this will hold the wings and legs close to the body.

Use a second piece of string and tie the ends of the legs close to the tail of the parson's nose. The trussing strings are easily cut at carving time and can be pulled out with one movement.

USING A SKEWER

A bird can be trussed with a skewer and string, although this method looks less attractive. Push the skewer through the bird below the thigh bone, and turn the bird on its breast. Catch the wing pinions in the string, and pass the string under the ends of the skewer and cross the pinions over the back of it. Turn the bird over, bring up string to secure the drumsticks, and tie round the parson's nose.

PREPARING THE GIBLETS

Discard the intestines. Split the gizzard and remove the thick inner membrane. Cut free the heart. Trim the neck and cut into two or three pieces. Remove any yellow-tinged pieces from the liver which may have been touched by the gall bladder. Wash well in cold water before use.

Boning a chicken

It is sometimes convenient to bone a chicken, using the skin and flesh as a casing for a savoury stuffing, and making a shape which is easy to cut for a buffet meal. This takes a little practice, but the only equipment necessary is a small sharp knife. Larger birds are easier to bone.

Remove trussing string and, with a sharp knife, slit the skin down the underside of the bird. Work the skin and flesh from the carcass with the knife until the leg joint is reached.

Work very carefully so that the skin is not split. Cut the sinew between the ball and socket joint which joins the thigh bone to the carcase. Hold the end of the joint and cut away the flesh, working from the inside of the leg. Scrape the thighbone clean and continue cleaning the drumstick until the whole leg bone is free of flesh. Take the leg bone from the carcase, and repeat the process on the other side.

Sever the wing joint from the carcase. With the knife, work down towards the breastbone. Free the other wing in the same way. Carefully cut away the skin from the top of the breastbone.

Spread the chicken flat and spread on the stuffing. Sew up and truss the bird into shape.

Spatchcocking

This method of preparing a small bird is used when it is to be grilled, and for this the bird is neatly flattened. Leave the pinions on the wings and push back the flesh of the legs so that the ends of the drumsticks are bared. Split the bird down the back without dividing in two. Open out and flatten the bird. Make a small slit at the base of each thigh, double back the legs and insert the bare bone into the slit. Fold the pinions back beneath the wings so that they are held flat. Secure the bird with two crossed skewers.

Carving

Poor carving can wreck a beautifully cooked chicken or turkey, producing ugly chunks of meat instead of thin neat slices. Follow the diagram below, but, to be sure of success, take one or two elementary steps. Put the bird on a large enough plate, board, or spiked carving dish, and try not to clutter the dish with too many accompaniments and trimmings. Give the carver room to manouevre, preferably on a side table, and provide a second dish on which slices may be placed as they are carved. Above all, have a really sharp knife and a fork with a finger-guard. For a large bird, an electric carving knife is useful, as large thin slices can be carved quickly and easily and the bird will provide far more portions than usual.

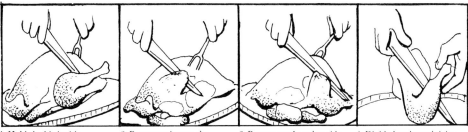

1. Hold the bird with carving fork and remove drumstick and thigh in one piece.

2. Remove wing on the same side and then slice breast.

3. Repeat on the other side.

4. Divide leg through joint which joins drumstick and thigh.

13

2   Roast Chicken

Roast chicken is a traditional favourite, but there are many variations on the basic dish. The bird may be simply roasted with herbs and seasoning, and a little oil and butter for basting during cooking. It may be filled with a herb and breadcrumb stuffing or with a combination of fruit, nuts, rice or sweetcorn. A third variation is a light stuffing combined with a glaze of fruit juice, honey or yoghurt which provides a crisp and delicious finish for the skin. A chicken may also be roasted in a clay chicken brick, and this method is dealt with at the end of this chapter. Additional ideas for stuffings are given in Chapter Three.

OVEN-ROASTING

Always make sure a frozen bird is completely thawed before cooking, and wash and wipe it well. Preheat the oven to 190°C (375°F)/Gas 5. Put the chicken in a roasting tin and brush it with melted butter or oil. A mixture of the two fats is excellent as the oil prevents the butter from burning. Put strips of streaky bacon over the breast and cook the chicken for 20 minutes per 450 g (1 lb) and 20 minutes over. Remove the bacon for the last 30 minutes and baste the bird to allow the chicken breast to become golden. Use the pan juices for making gravy after straining off excess fat. For a very juicy bird, put a knob of butter and some chopped fresh herbs into the body cavity and roast the bird breast downwards, allowing 20 minutes on each side and then turning upright for the remaining cooking time.

Birds can be stuffed in the neck end and in the body cavity, and this will help to keep the flesh moist and to extend servings. Be sure to calculate the weight of the stuffing with the bird and allow a longer cooking time so that the heat penetrates and cooks the bird and stuffing right through. Test all chickens when cooked by piercing the thick part of the bird near the thigh with a sharp knife – the juice should run clear without a pink tinge.

There is a slight variation between oven temperatures and cooking times in some of the following recipes to allow for different ingredients, eg, if a glaze contains honey it should not be cooked at a high temperature which can singe the skin.

Roast Chicken with Tarragon

1.5-kg (3¼-lb) chicken
50 g (2 oz) butter
30 ml (2 tablespoons) fresh
  tarragon leaves or 10 ml (2
  teaspoons) dried tarragon
1 clove garlic
salt and pepper
250 ml (½ pint) chicken stock
30 ml (2 tablespoons) brandy or
  sherry
60 ml (4 tablespoons) double
  cream

Truss the chicken neatly. Cream together the butter and tarragon. Crush the garlic and blend with the butter. Season well with salt and pepper. Spread some of the tarragon butter over the bird, placing the rest inside. Put the bird on its side on a grid in the roasting pan. Pour in the stock and cook at 200°C (400°F)/Gas 6 for 20 minutes. Turn the chicken on the other side, baste and roast for 20 minutes. Turn the bird breast side upwards, baste again and continue roasting for 20 minutes. Put the chicken on a heated serving dish and keep it warm. Remove the grid from the pan and pour off the fat, retaining the juices. Add brandy or sherry, bring to the boil, and stir in the cream. Season and pour into a warmed sauce-boat. This French method of cooking chicken with its own sauce, gives a delicate and delicious flavour. No other accompaniments are necessary, but the bird is good with croquette potatoes and beans.

Herb Chicken

1.5-kg (3¼-lb) chicken
100 g (4 oz) butter
15 ml (1 tablespoon) chopped
  parsley
30 ml (2 teaspoons) chopped
  thyme
10 ml (2 teaspoons) chopped
  rosemary
10 ml (2 teaspoons) chopped
  marjoram
1 clove garlic
grated rind of 1 lemon
salt and pepper

Cream the butter and mix it with the herbs, crushed garlic, lemon rind, salt and pepper. Spread this all over the chicken. Roast it at 180°C (350°F)/Gas 4 for 1½ hours. Serve with bacon rolls cooked in the oven for the last 15 minutes' cooking time, and with new potatoes, sweetcorn, peas and young carrots.

Orange Chicken

1.5-kg (3½-lb) chicken
salt and pepper
4 oranges
2 onions
3 sticks celery
100 g (4 oz) butter
5 slices bread
1 chicken stock cube
30 ml (2 tablespoons) chopped
  parsley
1 egg
60 ml (4 tablespoons) coarse-cut
  marmalade

Sprinkle the chicken inside and out with salt and pepper. Squeeze the juice from 1 orange and sprinkle this inside the bird. Chop the onions and celery and cook them in half the butter until soft and golden. Toast the bread to medium brown and cut it into cubes. Put these into a bowl with the crumbled stock cube, onions, celery, chopped orange flesh, parsley and beaten egg. Stuff the chicken with this mixture. Spread the marmalade on the breast of the chicken and dot it with the remaining butter. Roast at 190°C (375°F)/Gas 5 for 1¼ hours. Serve with watercress and straw potatoes.

Plum-Glazed Chicken

1.35-kg (3-lb) chicken
salt and pepper
450 g (1 lb) canned red plums
30 ml (2 tablespoons)
  concentrated orange juice
5 ml (1 teaspoon)
  Worcestershire sauce

Season the chicken with salt and pepper and put it in a roasting tin. Cut 3 plums into quarters and set them aside. Drain the remaining plums and reserve the syrup. Force the plums through a sieve and mix the pulp with syrup, orange juice and Worcestershire sauce. Brush the chicken with the plum glaze and bake it at 190°C (375°F)/Gas 5 for 1¼ hours, basting with the plum glaze three or four times during cooking. Heat the remaining glaze, pour it over the chicken and decorate it with the remaining plums. Serve with jacket potatoes or plain boiled potatoes.

Honey Roast Chicken

1.5-kg (3-lb) chicken
salt and pepper
1 cooking apple
1 large onion
60 ml (4 tablespoons) oil
60 ml (4 tablespoons) clear
  honey

Sprinkle the inside of the chicken with salt and pepper. Peel and core the apple and cut it into quarters. Put them inside the chicken together with the quartered onion. Brush it with a little oil and put it into a roasting tin. Pour over the honey and put the rest of the oil into the tin. Roast at 190°C (375°F)/Gas 5 for 1¼ hours, basting from time to time with the pan juices.

Glazed Chicken with Cherries

1.5-kg (3½-lb) chicken
45 ml (3 tablespoons) honey
50 g (2 oz) butter
5 ml (1 teaspoon) powdered
   rosemary
225 g (8 oz) sweet cherries
1 small crisp lettuce
50 g (2 oz) flaked almonds
60 ml (4 tablespoons) oil
30 ml (2 tablespoons) cider
   vinegar
salt and pepper

Mix together the honey, melted butter and rosemary. Place the chicken in a roasting tin, prick the breast well and brush the bird liberally with the honey and butter mixture. Spoon the rest of the mixture inside the carcase. Roast the chicken at 190°C (375°F)/Gas 6, for 1¼ hours, until it is golden brown. Let the chicken become cold. Prepare a serving dish with crisp lettuce leaves and stoned, halved cherries. Place the chicken on the dish and scatter it with the toasted almonds. Mix the oil, vinegar, salt and pepper, and pour this over the lettuce and cherries. The chicken can, of course, be served hot and is delicious with new potatoes and peas.

Algerian Stuffed Chicken

1.8-kg (4-lb) chicken
salt
100 g (4 oz) butter
1 medium onion

Stuffing:
40 g (1½ oz) raisins
25 g (1 oz) hot cooked rice
25 g (1 oz) butter
1 small onion
2.5 ml (½ teaspoon) ground
   ginger
pinch of curry powder
pinch of turmeric
pinch of basil
pinch of thyme
salt and pepper
15 ml (1 tablespoon) clear honey
15 ml (1 tablespoon) lemon juice
1 hard-boiled egg

Mix together the raisins, hot rice, butter, finely chopped onion, spices and herbs, salt, pepper, honey, lemon juice and mashed egg. Loosen the chicken skin from the breast and insert the stuffing evenly on each side between the skin and the flesh. Rub the outside of the chicken with salt and put butter on the skin in flakes. Put the bird into a roasting tin with the onion and add 125 ml (¼ pint) water. Roast at 190°C (375°F)/Gas 5 for 1½ hours, basting frequently.

Sunshine Chicken

1.35-kg (3-lb) chicken
salt and pepper
pinch of ground ginger
10 dried prunes
50 g (2 oz) butter
1 medium onion
grated rind of 1 orange
30 ml (2 tablespoons) sweet sherry

Season the chicken inside with salt, pepper and ginger. Put in the prunes and half the butter. Put the chicken into a roasting tin and spread the remaining butter over the breast. Season the breast with a little more salt, pepper and ginger. Slice the onion and put it into the roasting tin. Roast it at 190°C (375°F)/Gas 5 for 1½ hours. Cut the chicken into 4 pieces and put them on a serving dish. Arrange the prunes round the chicken and sprinkle it with the orange rind. Add the sherry to the pan juices, heat and stir and pour this over the chicken.

Tunisian Roast Chicken

1.5-kg (3½-lb) chicken
200 g (7 oz) long-grain rice
50 g (2 oz) butter
1 medium onion
1 chicken liver
50 g (2 oz) fresh dates
25 g (1 oz) currants
375 ml (¾ pint) water or chicken stock
15 m (3 teaspoons) salt
pepper
1 bayleaf
25 g (1 oz) melted butter
125 ml (¼ pint) natural yoghurt

Place the rice in a sieve and run hot water through it until the water runs clear. Melt 50 g (2 oz) butter in a saucepan and add the finely chopped onion. Cook for 5 minutes to soften, but not brown. Chop the chicken liver and add it to the pan with the stoned dates, cut into quarters. Cook for 2 minutes. Stir in the rice and cook until the rice absorbs the butter and begins to go opaque. Add the currants and water, or stock, 1½ teaspoons of salt and pepper, and the bayleaf. Bring this to the boil, reduce the heat, cover and cook gently for 25 minutes until all the liquid has been absorbed.

Fill the inside of the chicken with nearly half the rice mixture and the melted butter. Keep the remaining rice warm and covered to serve separately with the chicken. Truss the chicken and put it in a roasting dish. Mix the remaining 1½ teaspoons salt with the yoghurt and spread half of this mixture over the chicken. Roast at 200°C (400°F)/Gas 6 for 15 minutes, then spread the remaining yoghurt mixture over the chicken. Cover the roasting tin with cooking foil, lower the oven temperature to 180°C (350°F)/Gas 4 and cook for 1 hour. Fresh dates are widely available in greengrocers, and are very plump and juicy. If not available, use stoned boxed dates.

18

Nigerian Chicken

1.8-kg (4-lb) chicken
1 large onion
3 rashers streaky bacon
225 g (8 oz) peanut butter
15 g (½ oz) wholemeal flour
salt and pepper
desiccated coconut
salted peanuts

Simmer the chicken in water to cover it until it is tender. Slice the onion thinly and chop the bacon. Put the bacon into a thick-bottomed pan and cook it until the fat runs. Stir in the onion and cook it until soft and golden. Mix the peanut butter and flour and stir them in, together with 375 ml (¾ pint) cooking liquid from the chicken. Season with salt and pepper and simmer to make a creamy sauce. Cut the chicken flesh into large pieces and put them into a casserole. Pour on the sauce, cover and cook at 170°C (325°F)/Gas 3 for 45 minutes. Serve sprinkled with coconut and peanuts, together with boiled rice and chutney.

Moroccan Lemon Chicken

1.8-kg (4-lb) chicken
bunch of fresh herbs
60 ml (4 tablespoons) oil
65 kg (2½ oz) butter
1 lemon
40 g (1½ oz) raisins
pinch of saffron
pinch of ground allspice
5 ml (1 teaspoon) pepper
2.5 ml (½ teaspoon) curry
  powder
5 ml (1 teaspoon) salt
1.2 ml (¼ teaspoon) sugar

Cut the lemon in quarters and put it into a screwtop jar with the raisins, saffron, allspice, pepper, curry powder, salt and sugar. Cover, shake well and leave it to stand. Put the chicken into a pan with water to come three-quarters of the way up the chicken. Add a pinch of salt, herbs and oil, cover and bring it to the boil. Reduce the heat and simmer for 45 minutes. Take off the lid, increase the heat and cook for 20 minutes until the water has evaporated. Melt the butter in a roasting tin until it is just brown. Put the drained chicken into the tin and strain over the lemon liquid from the jar, retaining the lemon pieces. Roast it at 190°C (375°F)/Gas 5 for 15 minutes, basting with the pan juices. Just before serving, squeeze over the remaining liquid from the lemon pieces. Serve with rice or plain boiled potatoes.

Turkish Roast Chicken

1.8-kg (4-lb) chicken
25 g (1 oz) peanut kernels
25 g (1 oz) seedless raisins
100 g (4 oz) long-grain rice
100 g (4 oz) butter
salt and pepper
250 ml ($\frac{1}{2}$ pint) water

Chop the chicken giblets in small pieces. Soak the nuts and raisins in a little boiling water for 1 hour. Drain the nuts and raisins. Melt half the butter and toss the nuts, raisins, giblets and rice in it until golden. Salt and pepper well and pour in 250 ml ($\frac{1}{2}$ pint) boiling water. Cover and bring to the boil and then simmer for 25 minutes. Take off the lid and cook on a low heat until the rice becomes dry and shiny. Put this stuffing into the chicken and place it in a roasting tin. Spread the remaining butter on the chicken and sprinkle it with a little salt. Roast at 190°C (375°F)/Gas 5 for 1$\frac{1}{2}$ hours. Serve with a cucumber salad.

Chicken in Vermouth Sauce

1.8-kg (4-lb) chicken
2 sprigs fresh tarragon
50 g (2 oz) butter
salt and pepper
250 ml ($\frac{1}{2}$ pint) dry vermouth
125 ml ($\frac{1}{4}$ pint) single cream

Season the chicken inside and out and put the tarragon inside. Put half the butter inside also and spread the rest on the bird. Put it into a roasting tin and pour on half the vermouth. Roast at 200°C (400°F)/Gas 6 for 1$\frac{1}{4}$ hours, basting occasionally. Put the chicken on a serving dish. Drain the fat from the pan and stir the remaining vermouth and 2 tablespoons water into the pan juices. Simmer gently and stir in the cream. Season to taste and simmer until the sauce is reduced by one third. Carve the chicken and pour the sauce over before serving.

The Chicken Brick

A chicken brick is made of clay and needs some pre-treatment before use and careful treatment subsequently. It produces a delicious chicken with a distinctive flavour and rich juices.

Before using the chicken brick for the first time, soak it in cold water and scrub it well, but do not use detergent which will flavour the clay. If you like garlic, rub the inside of the brick with a cut clove each time before using it. Do not add fat to the bird, but brush the meat with a little oil before seasoning.

The brick should always be put in a cold oven set at a very high temperature — 250°C (500°F)/Gas 9. Allow 1½ hours for a bird weight of 1.35 kg (3 lb) and do not open the brick to baste as the bird will brown inside itself. Juice which forms in the brick can be strained to serve as gravy. The brick should be cleaned after use with plenty of hot water and 2 tablespoons of vinegar or salt.

Roast Chicken in the Brick

1.35-kg (3-lb) chicken
salt and pepper
15 ml (1 tablespoon) olive oil
3 sprigs parsley
1 clove garlic

Season the chicken inside and put in the parsley sprigs and chopped garlic. Brush the bird with oil and sprinkle it with salt and pepper. Put it in the brick and cook it for 1½ hours. Substitute thyme, rosemary, basil, tarragon or marjoram for the parsley if liked, but do not mix the herbs. Two sprigs will be enough of these stronger-tasting ones.

Lemon Chicken in the Brick

1.35-kg (3-lb) chicken
1 chicken liver
2 sprigs parsley
1 clove garlic
5 large mushrooms
½ lemon
salt and pepper
pinch of chopped marjoram
olive oil

Dip the liver in oil, season and sprinkle with marjoram. Put it inside the bird with the parsley, chopped garlic, quartered mushrooms and chopped lemon. Brush the chicken with oil and sprinkle on salt, pepper and more marjoram. Put the bird in the chicken brick and cook for 1½ hours.

21

Workman's Chicken in a Brick

1.35-kg (3-lb) chicken
25 g (1 oz) butter
grated rind of 1 lemon
225 g (8 oz) cooked ham
225 g (8 oz) mushrooms
225 g (8 oz) noodles
salt and pepper

Place the chicken in the brick. Spread the butter over it. Sprinkle over the grated lemon rind, shredded ham and chopped mushrooms. Season well. Cook for $1\frac{1}{2}$ hours. Serve on a bed of noodles.

3   Stuffings, Sauces and Accompaniments

A roast chicken or turkey would not be the same without some of the traditional accompaniments. Roast potatoes, a variety of vegetables and a richly flavoured gravy are considered essential. Most people expect a savoury stuffing with their poultry, and often a sauce is served as well. It makes a marathon for the cook, but the result is a feast instead of an everyday meal.

The best gravy is made with stock from the giblets, simmered while the bird is roasting. This can simply be added to the roasting juices in the tin, and some cooks like to add the finely chopped giblets too. A little wine may be added to this gravy and, if giblet stock is not available, water used from cooking the accompanying vegetables will be satisfactory. A few people like to add single cream to the pan juices, with only a little stock, to make a cream gravy which is particularly good with turkey.

Bread sauce is traditional with poultry, and cranberry sauce usually accompanies turkey, while some people also like a sharp apple sauce. All these can be made well in advance (frozen if necessary) and heated before serving time.

With these simple items out of the way, there can be concentration on the stuffing which can do so much to improve a bird which is rather bland. The purpose of stuffing is to enhance the flavour of poultry and also to extend the portions of meat. Stuffing absorbs cooking juices from the bird and should always be made very light in texture. Too often, a stuffing is made like a pudding, and by the time it has absorbed the bird's juices, it becomes a solid lump.

To achieve lightness, use day-old bread which can be rubbed into crumbs, or cut into very small cubes. Season well and only use just enough egg or other liquid to produce a light crumbly mixture which does not stick together. Stuff the bird with a light hand and do not ram in the filling in a tight parcel. While the body cavity of a chicken is traditionally stuffed, it is better to stuff only the neck cavity of a turkey so that heat penetrates right through the bird and it is completely cooked. If a second stuffing is needed for the turkey, this can be cooked separately, in the form of stuffing balls, in the tin with the turkey, or in a separate dish with added fat. If preferred, the stuffing may simply be placed in a thick layer in a second roasting tin, dotted with a little fat, to cook on the shelf beneath the bird.

For a change of flavour, include different herbs in the stuffing (sage, marjoram, thyme and rosemary are particularly fragrant and delicious), orange or lemon juice and grated rind, or dried fruit. If apricots or prunes are used, soak them overnight to plump them up

23

before cutting and adding to the stuffing; sultanas and raisins just need soaking in boiling water for a few minutes to get the same effect. For convenience, a packet stuffing can be used as the basis of a recipe, and can be quickly varied with a little dried fruit, some lemon rind, or a little sausagemeat, bacon, poultry liver or onion.

It is not recommended to stuff a bird before freezing, as the life of stuffing is only about 4 weeks, while poultry will keep for many months. In fact, it takes little time and trouble to make up stuffing while a bird is thawing. If you want to freeze stuffing, pack it separately in polythene bags for short-term storage. It will only take a couple of hours to thaw before stuffing the bird for roasting.

Each stuffing recipe in this chapter has been tested for a specific weight of bird. If you want to increase or decrease quantities, or make up your own flavour-combinations, allow about $\frac{1}{6}$ weight of the bird for the weight of stuffing, eg, for a bird weighing 1.5 kg ($3\frac{1}{2}$ lb) allow approximately 300 g (10 oz) stuffing.

Other ideas for stuffing are included in Chapter Two, as some roasting recipes require both stuffing and a complementary exterior treatment.

Cider Gravy

15 g ($\frac{1}{2}$ oz) butter
1 turkey or chicken liver
1 small onion
25 g (1 oz) plain flour
500 ml (1 pint) Strongbow cider
   (or another make of dry
   cider)
salt and pepper

Melt the butter and cook the whole liver until brown. Lift it out and reserve it. Chop the onion finely and cook it in the butter until soft and golden. Stir in the flour and cook for 2 minutes. Gradually add cider, salt and pepper and stir over a low heat until smooth and creamy. Put this through a sieve to remove the pieces of onion. When the bird has been cooked, drain the fat from the pan and add the pan juices to the gravy. Stir in the finely chopped liver and reheat.

Bacon Rolls

Use streaky bacon rashers and remove the rinds and any small bones. Stretch and flatten the bacon rashers with a flat-bladed knife so that they are very thin and long. Cut each one in half and roll it up firmly. Thread about a dozen bacon rolls onto a thin smooth skewer. Cook these under the grill or in the oven with the bird until just crisp. Remove from the skewer to serve round the bird.

Liver and Bacon Rolls

chicken or turkey liver
thin streaky bacon

Cut the liver into bite-sized pieces. Cut each bacon rasher in half and press it out thinly with a broad-bladed knife. Roll a piece of bacon round each piece of liver. Thread these on a skewer and cook them with the bird in the oven for 25 minutes.

Basic Poultry Stuffing

25 g (1 oz) butter
1 small onion
75 g (3 oz) breadcrumbs
1 lemon
salt and pepper
15 ml (1 tablespoon) chopped
  thyme
15 ml (1 tablespoon) chopped
  marjoram
10 ml (2 teaspoons) chopped
  parsley
1 egg

Melt the butter and cook the finely chopped onion until soft and golden. Add this to the breadcrumbs, grated lemon rind and juice, salt, pepper, herbs and egg. Enough for a 1.5-kg ($3\frac{1}{2}$-lb) chicken.

Bacon Stuffing

100 g (4 oz) streaky bacon
1 small onion
25 g (1 oz) butter
75 g (3 oz) fresh white
  breadcrumbs
30 ml (2 tablespoons) chopped
  parsley
pepper

Remove the rind and cut the bacon into pieces. Peel and chop the onion. Cook the bacon and onion for 4 minutes in the butter. Stir in the breadcrumbs, chopped parsley and pepper. Enough for a 1.5-kg ($3\frac{1}{2}$-lb) chicken (double or treble for a turkey).

Herb and Liver Stuffing

25 g (1 oz) butter
1 shallot
50 g (2 oz) breadcrumbs
5 ml (1 teaspoon) chopped
    tarragon
5 ml (1 teaspoon) chopped
    chervil
salt and pepper
1 chicken liver

Melt the butter and cook the finely chopped shallot until soft and golden. Add the butter and shallot to the breadcrumbs with the herbs, seasoning and finely chopped chicken liver. Enough for a 1.5-kg (3½-lb) chicken.

Liver Stuffing

1 turkey liver
50 g (2 oz) lamb's liver
1 rasher streaky bacon
1 medium onion
1 clove garlic
25 g (1 oz) shredded suet
100 g (4 oz) breadcrumbs
5 ml (1 teaspoon) chopped
    parsley
2.5 ml (½ teaspoon) thyme
2.5 ml (½ teaspoon) lemon
    juice
salt and pepper
1 egg

Chop the turkey and lamb's livers, bacon and onion. Crush the garlic clove. Mix this with all the other ingredients. Use the stuffing for the neck cavity of a turkey. The same stuffing may be used inside a chicken, substituting the chicken liver for turkey liver.

Mushroom Stuffing

100 g (4 oz) mushrooms
1 small onion
25 g (1 oz) butter
30 ml (2 tablespoons) chopped
    parsley
salt and pepper
50 g (2 oz) breadcrumbs
1 egg

Chop the mushrooms and onion very finely, then fry them in the hot butter for a few minutes. Add the chopped parsley, seasoning and breadcrumbs and mix well. Moisten with a little beaten egg. Enough for a 1.5-kg (3½-lb) chicken.

26

Sweetcorn Stuffing

25 g (1 oz) butter
1 small onion
150 g (5 oz) canned sweetcorn
grated rind of ½ lemon
squeeze of lemon juice
15 ml (1 tablespoon) chopped
   parsley
salt and pepper
1 egg

Melt the butter and cook the finely chopped onion until soft and golden. Stir this into the sweetcorn kernels with the lemon rind and juice, parsley, salt, pepper and egg. Enough for a 1.5-kg (3½-lb) chicken. A little bacon may be cooked with the onion and added to the stuffing if liked.

Pork and Prune Stuffing

100 g (4 oz) prunes
75 ml (3 fl oz) white wine
175 g (6 oz) lean pork
1 small onion
1 egg yolk
15 ml (1 tablespoon) brandy
salt and pepper
15 ml (1 tablespoon) chopped
   parsley
pinch of thyme

Soak the prunes in the wine overnight. Stone them and mash them in the wine to make a purée. Mix this with the minced pork and onion and add the egg yolk, brandy, salt, pepper, parsley and thyme. Enough for a 1.5-kg (3½-lb) chicken, or the neck cavity of a small turkey.

Lemon and Mushroom Stuffing

225 g (8 oz) breadcrumbs
175 g (6 oz) shredded suet
10 ml (2 teaspoons) thyme
1 lemon
salt and pepper
pinch of nutmeg
100 g (4 oz) mushrooms
100 g (4 oz) streaky bacon
25 g (1 oz) butter
2 eggs

Mix together the breadcrumbs, suet and thyme. Add the grated rind and juice of the lemon, salt, pepper and nutmeg. Chop the mushrooms and bacon and cook them in the butter until the bacon is just golden and the mushrooms are soft. Add this to the breadcrumb mixture with the beaten eggs. Enough for a 2.2–3.6-kg (5–8-lb) chicken or turkey.

Chestnut Stuffing

450 g (1 lb) chestnuts
250 ml (½ pint) stock or milk
50 g (2 oz) bacon
100 g (4 oz) breadcrumbs
10 ml (2 teaspoons) chopped
  parsley
25 g (1 oz) butter
pinch of grated lemon rind
salt and pepper
pinch of sugar
1 egg

Make a slit in both ends of the chestnuts and boil them in water for about 10 minutes. Take a few at a time from the water and skin them. Put the shelled nuts into a pan with enough stock or milk just to cover and simmer them gently until tender. Mash the chestnuts. Pound this with the finely chopped bacon, then add the breadcrumbs, parsley, melted butter and lemon rind. Season and bind with the beaten egg. Enough for a 2.2–3.6-kg (5–8-lb) chicken or the neck cavity of a turkey.

Chestnut and Orange Stuffing

225 g (8 oz) chestnuts
25 g (1 oz) butter
1 large onion
100 g (4 oz) long-grain rice
2 oranges
1 bayleaf
salt and pepper
1 egg

Make a slit in both ends of the chestnuts and boil them in water for about 10 minutes. Take a few at a time from the water and skin them. Melt the butter and cook the chopped onion until soft. Cook the rice in boiling salted water for 6 minutes and drain well. Mix the rice, onion and chopped chestnuts. Cut the oranges in half and scoop out the flesh without any pith. Add the orange pieces to the rice, with the bayleaf, seasonings and egg. Enough for a 1.5-kg (3½-lb) chicken or the neck cavity of a turkey.

Chestnut and Sausage Stuffing

450 g (1 lb) cooked chestnuts
450 g (1 lb) sausage meat
1 medium onion
25 g (1 oz) butter
3 sticks celery
2 eggs
125 ml (¼ pint) milk or stock
salt and pepper

To prepare the chestnuts, slit them at both ends and boil them in water until soft, then peel and mash them. (Canned cooked chestnuts may be used instead.) Mix them with the sausagemeat. Chop the onion finely and cook it in butter until soft and golden. Add the finely chopped celery and stir for 1 minute. Put the onion and celery into the chestnut mixture and mix it with the beaten eggs, milk or stock, salt and pepper. Enough for a 2.2–3.6-kg (5–8-lb) chicken or the neck cavity of a turkey.

Sausage Stuffing

25 g (1 oz) dripping
1 large onion
450 g (1 lb) pork sausagemeat
salt and pepper
90 ml (6 tablespoons) fresh
  breadcrumbs
10 ml (2 teaspoons) chopped
  parsley
5 ml (1 teaspoon) mixed herbs

Melt the dripping. Chop the onion and mix it with the sausagemeat. Cook the sausagemeat and onion lightly in the dripping for a few minutes, until just coloured. Mix in the other ingredients. Enough for a 2.2–3.6-kg (5–8-lb) chicken or turkey.

Savoury Sausage Stuffing

675 g (1½ lb) pork sausagemeat
10 ml (2 teaspoons) chopped
  mixed herbs
1 large onion
1 egg

Put the sausagemeat and herbs in a bowl and mix them with a fork so that the herbs are well distributed. Chop the onions finely and work them into the sausagemeat with the beaten egg. Enough for a 2.2–3.6-kg (5–8-lb) chicken or turkey.

Sausage and Rum Stuffing

225-g (8-oz) packet herb-
  seasoned bread stuffing
225 g (8 oz) pork sausagemeat
45 ml (3 tablespoons) single
  cream
45 ml (3 tablespoons) rum

Make up the herb stuffing as instructed on the packet. Mix this with the sausagemeat, cream and rum and blend it all well together. Enough for a 2.2–3.6-kg (5–8 lb) chicken or turkey.

Celery and Sausage Stuffing

4 sticks celery
1 small onion
5 ml (1 teaspoon) mixed herbs
15 g (½ oz) butter
350 g (12 oz) pork sausagemeat
squeeze of lemon juice

Chop the celery and onion finely and soften them, with the herbs, in the butter. Add this to the sausagemeat with lemon juice and mix well. Enough for a 1.5-kg (3½-lb) chicken. (Double or treble the stuffing for a turkey.)

29

Celery Stuffing

75 g (3 oz) lean bacon
1 stick celery
leaves from a head of celery
25 g (1 oz) mushrooms
25 g (1 oz) fresh breadcrumbs
1 egg yolk
salt and pepper

Chop the bacon and fry it until it is crisp. Drain it and mix it with the chopped celery, chopped celery leaves, roughly chopped mushrooms and the breadcrumbs. Bind the stuffing together with sufficient of the egg yolk and season well. Enough for a 1.5-kg (3½-lb) chicken. (Double or treble the stuffing for a turkey.)

Almond and Raisin Stuffing

25 g (1 oz) butter
1 medium onion
100 g (4 oz) long-grain rice
100 g (4 oz) liver sausage
50 g (2 oz) almonds
50 g (2 oz) raisins
grated rind of 1 orange
2.5 ml (½ teaspoon) Tabasco
   sauce
salt and pepper
1 egg

Melt the butter and fry the finely chopped onion until soft and golden. Cook the rice in boiling salted water for 6 minutes, and drain well. Mix the onion, rice, chopped liver sausage, chopped almonds, raisins, grated orange rind, sauce, seasoning and egg and mix well. Enough for a 1.5-kg (3½-lb) chicken or for the neck cavity of a turkey.

Cranberry and Prune Stuffing

175 g (6 oz) prunes
30 ml (2 tablespoons) cranberry
   sauce
1 cooking apple
40 g (1½ oz) almonds
100 g (4 oz) breadcrumbs
½ lemon
1 egg
15 ml (1 tablespoon) oil
salt and pepper

Soak the prunes overnight and then drain and chop them. Mix them with the cranberry sauce (for preference use a whole-berry sauce). Peel, core and chop the apple. Blanch and chop the almonds. Mix the apple and almonds with the prunes and add the breadcrumbs, grated lemon rind and juice, egg, oil and seasoning. Enough for the neck cavity of a turkey. This stuffing is also delicious with chicken.

Apricot and Sultana Stuffing

50 g (2 oz) dried apricots
25 g (1 oz) sultanas
75 g (3 oz) fresh white
   breadcrumbs
pinch of ground mixed spice
salt and pepper
15 ml (1 tablespoon) lemon juice
25 g (1 oz) butter
1 egg

Soak the dried apricots in cold water overnight and then drain and chop them. Pour boiling water over the sultanas and leave them for 3 minutes. Drain and mix the sultanas with the apricots and breadcrumbs. Stir in the seasonings, lemon juice and melted butter and bind this together with beaten egg. Enough for a 1.5-kg (3½-lb) chicken. (Double or treble the stuffing for a turkey.)

Apricot and Rice Stuffing

175 g (6 oz) long-grain rice
1 turkey liver
1 large onion
75 g (3 oz) butter
225 g (8 oz) canned apricots
100 g (4 oz) almonds
45 ml (3 tablespoons) chopped
   parsley
5 ml (1 teaspoon) ground mixed
   spice
salt and pepper
1 egg yolk

Put the rice into boiling salted water and cook it for 6 minutes. Drain well. Chop the turkey liver and onion and fry them in the butter until the onion is soft and golden. Drain the apricots, reserving the juice. Chop the apricots and mix them with the rice, liver, onion, chopped almonds, parsley, spice, seasonings and egg yolk. Use this for the neck cavity of a turkey. Use the reserved apricot juice for basting the bird during cooking.

Spiced Fruit Stuffing

100 g (4 oz) seedless raisins
1 cooking apple
15 ml (1 tablespoon) chutney
2.5 ml (¼ teaspoon)
   Worcestershire sauce
50 g (2 oz) breadcrumbs
1 egg
salt and pepper

Put the raisins in a basin. Peel, core and chop the apple. Mix this with the raisins, chutney, sauce, breadcrumbs, egg and seasoning. Enough for a 1.5-kg (3½-lb) chicken, or the neck cavity of a turkey.

Celery and Herb Stuffing

2 sticks celery
1 small onion
15 ml (1 tablespoon) chopped
  parsley
15 ml (1 teaspoon) chopped mint
grated rind of ½ lemon
50 g (2 oz) butter
100 g (4 oz) breadcrumbs
1 egg
salt and pepper

Chop the celery and onion finely. Mix them with the herbs, lemon rind, melted butter, breadcrumbs, egg and seasoning. Enough for a 1.5-kg (3½-lb) chicken or the neck cavity of a turkey.

Spanish Olive Chicken

75 g (3 oz) stuffed green olives
75 g (3 oz) white bread
45 ml (3 tablespoons) milk
100 g (4 oz) cooked ham
1 egg
15 ml (1 tablespoon) chopped
  parsley
2.5 ml (½ teaspoon) salt
2.5 ml (½ teaspoon) made
  mustard
pepper

Chop half the olives and leave the rest whole. Cut the bread into cubes and soak them in milk, then squeeze dry. Chop the ham finely and mix together all the ingredients. Enough for a 1.5-kg (3½-lb) chicken. (Double or treble the stuffing for a turkey.)

Pineapple and Walnut Stuffing

40 g (1½ oz) butter
50 g (2 oz) stale white
  breadcrumbs
100 g (4 oz) canned pineapple
50 g (2 oz) walnuts
5 ml (1 teaspoon) salt
rind of ½ lemon

Melt the butter in a saucepan, add the breadcrumbs and cook, stirring, for 2 minutes. Drain and chop the pineapple and chop the walnuts. Stir in all the remaining ingredients and, if required, add a little pineapple juice to give a moist consistency. Enough for a 1.5-kg (3½-lb) chicken. (Double or treble the stuffing for a turkey.)

Bread Sauce

250 ml (½ pint) milk
1 small onion
6 cloves
1 blade of mace
50 g (2 oz) white breadcrumbs
25 g (1 oz) butter
salt and pepper
30 ml (2 tablespoons) single
    cream

Put the milk into a pan. Add the onion, stuck with cloves, and the mace. Heat this to boiling point. Take off the heat and leave to stand for 30 minutes. Strain off the milk and return it to the pan with the breadcrumbs and butter. Reheat gently, stirring well, and season to taste. Just before serving, stir in the cream.

Some people like pieces of onion in the sauce. In this case, simmer the milk and onion until the onion is tender. Remove the cloves and mace and chop the onion finely. Return them to the milk with the breadcrumbs and butter, and finish with the cream.

Celery Sauce

1 head of celery
stock
salt and pepper
pinch of ground nutmeg
15 g (½ oz) butter
15 g (½ oz) plain flour
250 ml (½ pint) single cream

Wash and trim the celery and chop it finely. Simmer it in chicken, turkey or giblet stock to cover, until soft. Strain the celery and rub it through a sieve, or blend it to a purée. Season well with salt, pepper and nutmeg. Work the butter and flour together to form a ball. Heat the cream gently and stir in the butter and flour. Cook very gently until thickened. Add the celery and heat without boiling, stirring well. Celery sauce used to be a popular accompaniment to boiled turkey, but it is equally good with roast or boiled chicken or roast turkey.

Cranberry Sauce

450 g (1 lb) cranberries
375 ml (¾ pint) water
350 g (12 oz) sugar

Rinse the cranberries. Melt the sugar in the water over a low heat. Add the cranberries and cook gently for about 15 minutes until the cranberries pop. The sauce may be served as it is, or may be sieved to give a smooth sauce.

Cranberry Orange Relish

225 g (8 oz) cranberries
1 orange
225 g (8 oz) sugar

Rinse the cranberries. Peel the orange and separate the segments. Mince or blend the cranberries and orange together. Stir in the sugar until it has dissolved. Store it in the refrigerator if all the relish is not used at one time.

Cranberry Apple Sauce

450 g (1 lb) cranberries
450 g (1 lb) cooking apples
500 ml (1 pint) water
175 g (6 oz) sugar

Rinse the cranberries. Peel and core the apples and cut them in slices. Put the apples and cranberries into a pan with water and sugar and simmer until the fruit is completely soft. Sieve or blend in a liquidizer and reheat to serve. A pinch of ground cinnamon is a delicious addition.

Apple and Lemon Sauce

450 g (1 lb) cooking apples
25 g (1 oz) butter
1.2 ml (¼ teaspoon) grated
   lemon rind
squeeze of lemon juice
5 ml (1 teaspoon) sugar

Peel and core the apples and cut them in thin slices. Melt the butter and stir in the apple slices. Cook very slowly until soft. Season with lemon rind, juice and sugar, and serve hot or cold. If possible use apples such as Bramleys seedlings which will cook to a soft pulp. No additional liquid should be necessary for the apples, but 1–2 tablespoons cider may be used if liked.

Mushroom Sauce

1 medium onion
15 g (½ oz) butter
175 g (6 oz) mushrooms
125 ml (¼ pint) red wine
125 ml (¼ pint) stock
15 g (½ oz) cornflour
15 ml (1 tablespoon)
   Worcestershire sauce
salt and pepper

Chop the onion finely and cook it in the butter until soft and golden. Chop the mushrooms and stir these with the onion for 2 minutes. Add the wine and stock and simmer for 10 minutes. Cool slightly and blend this in a liquidizer until smooth. Return it to the pan. Mix the cornflour with 1 tablespoon water and stir it into the sauce with the Worcestershire sauce, salt and pepper. Simmer this for 5 minutes and serve it hot with grilled or fried chicken, chicken loaf or chicken pie.

Indonesian Sauce

15 ml (1 tablespoon) salad oil
60 ml (4 tablespoons) peanut
   butter
125 ml ($\frac{1}{4}$ pint) tomato sauce
45 ml (3 tablespoons)
   Worcestershire sauce
1 clove garlic
large pinch of salt

Heat the oil gently and stir in the peanut butter. Continue heating and stirring until the peanut butter begins to thicken and darken slightly. Crush the garlic clove. Take the sauce off the heat and mix it very thoroughly with remaining ingredients. Leave it to stand for 2 hours. Reheat to serve with grilled or fried chicken, or kebabs.

Sweet and Sour Sauce

250 ml ($\frac{1}{2}$ pint) water
40 g (1$\frac{1}{2}$ oz) sugar
10 ml (2 teaspoons) soy sauce
30 ml (2 tablespoons) vinegar
10 ml (2 teaspoons) tomato
   purée
pinch of salt
75 g (3 oz) canned pineapple
1 small onion
15 g ($\frac{1}{2}$ oz) cornflour

Simmer the water and sugar together until the sugar has dissolved. Add the soy sauce, vinegar, tomato purée and salt. Drain the pineapple and chop it finely. Chop the onion finely also. Put these into the sauce and simmer for 10 minutes. Mix the cornflour with a little water and stir it into the sauce. Simmer and stir for 3 minutes. This is a useful sauce in which chopped cooked chicken can be heated to serve over rice as an emergency meal.

4   Whole-bird Casseroles

A whole chicken may be cooked in a casserole, or poached in water or stock and served with a sauce. In earlier days, a boiling fowl would have been used for this type of dish, but these are no longer widely available, and an oven-ready roasting bird will have to be used instead. If a boiling fowl is available, the same recipes may be followed, but longer cooking time should be allowed to allow for the extra toughness and greater weight of the bird. These recipes have been tested with birds weighing 1.35–1.5 kg (3–3½ lb) as these are easily bought from butchers and freezer cabinets. I normally use a larger bird, as chicken leftovers are always so good, and you can do the same, allowing a little longer for cooking if the bird is not tender. Always check the cooking time of casseroled birds carefully, as today's prepared chickens are very tender and if they are over-cooked the flesh quickly comes away from the bones – flavour will still be good but the finished dish does not look so presentable.

Some of the recipes require a bird to be poached in liquid. This indicates that the liquid should be warm when the chicken is added, then brought to the boil, and finally reduced to simmering for the full cooking time. The pan should be covered during cooking. The resulting stock can be used in the dish, and there is usually enough for a good soup too. One of today's oven-ready birds will take about 1¼–1½ hours to become tender. An old-fashioned boiling fowl will take 3–4 hours.

For a good-flavoured stock, add a bunch of fresh herbs, a few peppercorns, a couple of cloves, a carrot, onion and celery stick to the water. Salt is not usually added as the stock can become very salty if later reduced. A chicken cooked in this way is delicious with other meat such as ham or tongue, and with rice. Mushroom, cheese or celery sauces are all good accompaniments, or the stock may be made into a rich brown gravy.

Chicken cooked in a casserole in the oven may be accompanied by plenty of vegetables and gravy, and is, in effect, a stew. Some recipes use little liquid in the cooking and are then really pot-roasted, so that in appearance they are like roast chicken, but are very succulent and have a delicious sauce ready to serve with them. A heavy cast-iron casserole is useful for these whole-bird dishes, as cooking often needs to be begun on top of the stove and then continued in the oven.

Cider Chicken

1.5-kg (3½-lb) chicken
salt and pepper
1 clove garlic
25 g (1 oz) butter
30 ml (2 tablespoons) oil
2 medium onions
225 g (8 oz) tomatoes
25 g (1 oz) black olives
15 g (½ oz) plain flour
30 ml (2 tablespoons) tomato
   purée

Sprinkle the chicken with salt and pepper and rub it all over with the crushed garlic. Brown it on all sides in the butter and oil and put it into a casserole. Skin the tomatoes and slice them. Put them into the casserole with the sliced onions and stoned olives. Pour on the cider. Cover and cook at 190°C (375°F)/Gas 5 for 1½ hours. Strain the liquid into a saucepan. Mix the flour with a little water and stir it into the saucepan with the tomato purée. Bring this to the boil and simmer for 5 minutes, stirring well. Pour it over the chicken and vegetables.

Normandy Chicken

1.5-kg (3½-lb) chicken
100 g (4 oz) butter
675 g (1½ lb) eating apples
75 ml (3 fl oz) double cream
salt and pepper

Season the chicken and brown it all over in the butter. Peel the apples and cut them in thin slices. Put half the apples in a casserole. Pour half the butter over them and put in the chicken. Put in the remaining apples and pour on the rest of the butter. Cover and cook at 180°C (350°F)/Gas 4 for 45 minutes. Stir in the cream, cover, and continue cooking for 45 minutes. A pinch of cinnamon stirred in with the cream gives a delicious flavour to this dish.

Pot-Roast Chicken

1.35-kg (3-lb) chicken
40 g (1½ oz) butter
2 sticks celery
6 small onions
2 medium carrots
1 small turnip
250 ml (½ pint) chicken stock
salt and pepper
15 ml (1 tablespoon) chopped
   parsley

Brown the chicken lightly on all sides in the butter. Add the sliced vegetables, stock and seasoning. Cover and simmer for 2 hours, basting sometimes with the stock. Garnish with chopped parsley before serving. If preferred, the chicken may be cooked in the oven at 180°C (350°F)/Gas 4.

Chicken in the Pot

1.35-kg (3-lb) chicken
salt and pepper
50 g (2 oz) butter
100 g (4 oz) sausagemeat
15 ml (1 tablespoon) fresh
   breadcrumbs
1 chicken liver
15 ml (1 tablespoon) chopped
   parsley
15 ml (1 tablespoon) oil
100 g (4 oz) streaky bacon
   rashers or 6 slices bacon
12 button or baby onions
450 g (1 lb) potatoes

Take out the giblets and season the chicken inside and out with salt and pepper. Mix together the sausage-meat, breadcrumbs, chopped liver and parsley and stuff the neck of the bird with it, securing the flap of skin under the wing-tips. Heat the butter and oil and brown the chicken all over in it. Add the chopped bacon and whole onions, cover closely and cook over a very gentle heat for 15 minutes. Baste the chicken, add the potatoes, cut into small cubes, and turn them in the fat. Replace the lid and cook at 180°C (350°F)/Gas 4 for 1½ hours.

Chicken and Spicy Cabbage

1.5-kg (3½-lb) chicken
45 ml (3 tablespoons) oil
1 medium onion
4 rashers streaky bacon
750 g (1½ lb) red cabbage
15 ml (1 tablespoon) cornflour
125 ml (¼ pint) chicken stock
125 ml (¼ pint) cider
45 ml (3 tablespoons)
   Worcestershire sauce
30 ml (2 tablespoons) vinegar
25 g (1 oz) soft brown sugar
1 cooking apple

Heat the oil in a large cast-iron casserole and brown the chicken lightly on all sides. Lift the chicken from the casserole. Chop the onion and bacon and fry them in the oil until the onion is soft and golden. Stir in the finely shredded cabbage and remove the pan from the heat. Mix the cornflour with a little chicken stock and then put it into a saucepan with all the remaining ingredients, except the apple. Bring this to the boil, stirring well until thickened. Pour it into the cabbage. Put the chicken on top of the cabbage and cover the pan with a lid. Cook at 190°C (375°F)/Gas 5 for 1¼ hours.

Peel, core and slice the apple and add the slices to the cabbage. Continue cooking for 30 minutes. Serve with jacket potatoes baked in the oven. If you do not have a casserole which can be heated on top of the stove or in the oven, use a frying pan for the first part, and then transfer the ingredients to an ovenware dish to complete cooking.

Pot-Roast Paprika Chicken

1.5-kg (3½-lb) chicken
25 g (1 oz) paprika
salt and pepper
15 ml (1 tablespoon) wine
    vinegar
6 carrots
450 g (1 lb) small potatoes
250 ml (½ pint) stock
4 tomatoes
125 ml (¼ pint) yoghurt

Put the chicken into an ovenware dish. Mix the paprika, salt, pepper and vinegar and spread it over the chicken. Cut the carrots in thick slices and put them round the bird. Add the peeled potatoes (scrubbed new potatoes are particularly delicious in this dish). Pour on the stock. Cover and cook at 190°C (375°F)/Gas 5 for 45 minutes. Add the halved tomatoes and continue cooking for 30 minutes. Strain off the liquid and mix it with yoghurt. Season if necessary, reheat gently, and pour this over the chicken and vegetables.

Normandy Farm Chicken

2.2-kg (5-lb) boiling chicken
450 g (1 lb) eating apples
1 large onion
salt and pepper
500 ml (1 pint) apple juice

Peel and core the apples and cut them in thick slices. Stuff the bird with the pieces of apple. Put the chicken into a large casserole and arrange sliced onion round it. Season well with salt and pepper. Pour over the apple juice. Cover and cook at 170°C (325°F)/Gas 3 for 4–5 hours, until the chicken is tender. Serve the chicken with spoonfuls of onion and apple, with the pan juices as gravy. If a thicker sauce is wished, put 2 egg yolks into a bowl and pour in a little of the hot cooking liquid, whisking well. Stir this mixture into the remaining cooking liquid, but do not boil it.

Duke's Chicken

1.8-kg (4-lb) chicken
salt and pepper
sprig of basil
sprig of tarragon
sprig of parsley
pinch of ground coriander
100 g (4 oz) butter
100 ml (4 fl oz) dry vermouth
100 ml (4 fl oz) double cream

Salt and pepper the chicken inside and out. Keep one or two basil leaves aside, and put the remaining basil, tarragon, parsley and coriander inside the bird. Spread the butter all over the chicken and roast it at 190°C (375°F)/Gas 5 for 1½ hours. Remove the chicken from the roasting tin and keep it warm.

Pour the vermouth into the pan juices and mix well, scraping all the juices from the pan. Stir in the cream and heat it very gently. Add the remaining basil leaves, chopped very finely. Carve the chicken and arrange the pieces on a serving dish. Pour over the sauce and serve at once.

Somerset Chicken

1.35-kg (3-lb) chicken
100 g (4 oz) parsley and thyme
  stuffing (from a packet)
15 ml (1 tablespoon) soft dark
  brown sugar
rind of ½ lemon
5 ml (1 teaspoon) lemon juice
25 g (1 oz) butter
225 g (8 oz) cooking apples
125 ml (¼ pint) cider
10 ml (2 teaspoons) cornflour
30 ml (2 tablespoons) water
salt and pepper

Stuff the chicken with the parsley and thyme stuffing. Mix the sugar, lemon rind and juice and butter and spread the mixture on the breast of the chicken. Roast at 190°C (375°F)/Gas 5, basting frequently for 1¼ hours. Peel and core the apples and cut them into rings. Put the apple rings round the chicken and pour the cider over it. Continue cooking for 20 minutes. Put the chicken and apple rings on to a serving dish. Mix the cornflour and water until smooth and add it to the pan juices. Stir well, season, and bring to the boil. Serve each portion of chicken with some apple rings, stuffing and cider sauce.

Hawaiian Chicken

1.35-kg (3-lb) chicken
2 medium onions
1 bayleaf
2 cloves
400 g (14 oz) long-grain rice
75 g (3 oz) butter
2.5 ml (½ teaspoon) salt
10 ml (2 teaspoons) curry
  powder
50 g (2 oz) plain flour
125 ml (¼ pint) double cream
30 ml (2 tablespoons) dry sherry
425-g (15-oz) can pineapple
  chunks

Put the chicken into a large saucepan with one of the onions, the bayleaf and the cloves. Cover with water and simmer for 1½ hours. Leave the chicken to cool in the stock. Remove the skin and cut the chicken flesh into bite-sized pieces. Put the bones back in the cooking liquid and simmer for 20 minutes, then strain off the stock. Keep 500 ml (1 pint) chicken stock on one side, and cook the rice in the rest of the stock. Drain the rice and keep it hot. Meanwhile, fry the second chopped onion in the butter until it is just soft and golden. Work in the salt, curry powder and flour and gradually add the reserved chicken stock. Stir over a low heat until the sauce thickens. Remove it from the heat and stir in the cream, chicken pieces and sherry. Reheat very gently. Heat the pineapple chunks in their juice, drain them and add them to the chicken mixture. Serve the chicken in the sauce on top of the rice, with chutney as an accompaniment.

Henry IV's Chicken

1.5 kg (3½ lb) chicken
stock
1 bayleaf
900 g (2 lb) carrots
900 g (2 lb) turnips
900 g (2 lb) potatoes
1 cabbage
25 g (1 oz) butter
25 g (1 oz) plain flour
salt and pepper
1 clove garlic

Poach the chicken with the bayleaf in enough stock to cover for 1¼ hours. Peel the carrots, turnips and potatoes and add them to the chicken 20 minutes before it is cooked. Cut the cabbage in 8 pieces and cook it for 15 minutes. Place the chicken on a serving dish with the vegetables around it. Melt the butter, stir in the flour and cook gently for 1 minute. Blend in 500 ml (1 pint) stock in which the chicken and vegetables have been cooked. Add the crushed garlic, thicken over the heat, stirring constantly, and season well. Pour a little of the sauce over the bird before serving and serve the rest separately.

Chicken with Barbecue Sauce

1.35-kg (3-lb) chicken
50 g (2 oz) butter
30 ml (2 tablespoons) vinegar
15 ml (1 tablespoon)
  Worcestershire sauce
15 ml (1 tablespoon) tomato
  purée
1 small onion
1 clove garlic
5 ml (1 teaspoon) paprika
salt and pepper

Spread half the butter on the chicken and roast it at 190°C (375°F)/Gas 5 for 1¼ hours. Melt the remaining butter in a pan and add the vinegar, Worcestershire sauce, tomato purée, finely chopped onion, crushed garlic, paprika, salt and pepper. Bring this to the boil and simmer for 3 minutes. Ten minutes before the chicken is ready, brush it with the sauce and baste it once or twice. Serve it with the sauce and a salad.

Rissington Chicken

1.5-kg (3½-lb) chicken
225 g (8 oz) onions
450 g (1 lb) cooking apples
50 g (2 oz) butter
250 ml (½ pint) cider or stock
25 g (1 oz) pickling spice
15 ml (1 tablespoon) black
  treacle
1 clove garlic

Slice the onions. Peel and quarter the apples. Cook the onions in the butter until they are soft and golden. Put the apples in a casserole and then the chicken. Cover it with the onions and pour in the cider or stock. Cover and cook at 180°C (350°F)/Gas 4 for 45 minutes. Add the pickling spice tied in a piece of muslin, together with the crushed garlic and black treacle. Cover and continue cooking for 45 minutes. Take out the chicken and remove the pickling spice. Sieve the contents of the casserole, reheat and pour this over the chicken to serve.

Crisp Chicken and Rice

1.5-kg (3½-lb) chicken
salt and pepper
pinch of mustard powder
30 ml (2 tablespoons) oil
1 medium onion
25 g (1 oz) butter
liver from the chicken
250 ml (½ pint) beef consommé
250 ml (½ pint) water
175 g (6 oz) long-grain rice
10 ml (2 teaspoons)
  Worcestershire sauce

Sprinkle salt, pepper and mustard on the chicken and rub on the oil. Roast it at 190°C (375°F)/Gas 5 for 1 hour 25 minutes, basting frequently. Chop the onion finely and fry it in the butter until soft and golden. Add the chopped liver and cook for 1 minute. Add the consommé and the water and bring this to the boil. Put in the rice and cook for 12–15 minutes until it is tender and the liquid absorbed. Stir in the Worcestershire sauce with salt and pepper to taste. Carve the chicken and serve it with the rice and a green salad.

Chicken in Tomato Sauce

1.5-kg (3½-lb) chicken
3 medium onions
30 ml (2 tablespoons) olive oil
25 g (1 oz) plain flour
1 bayleaf
375 ml (¾ pint) tomato juice
250 ml (½ pint) stock
salt and pepper
chopped parsley

Poach the chicken in water for 1¼ hours and leave it to cool in the liquid. Slice the onions and cook them in the oil until soft and golden. Stir in the flour and cook for 1 minute. Add the bayleaf, tomato juice and stock from the chicken. Season well and simmer for 15 minutes until it is thick and creamy. Joint the cooked chicken and add it to the sauce. Heat gently and serve sprinkled with plenty of parsley.

Covent Garden Chicken

1.35-kg (3-lb) chicken
salt and pepper
100 g (4 oz) butter
12 baby carrots
4 baby white turnips
5 ml (1 teaspoon) sugar
8 button or baby onions
8 small new potatoes
100 g (4 oz) lean bacon
125 ml (¼ pint) chicken stock
125 ml (¼ pint) white wine

Season the chicken with salt and pepper. Melt half the butter in a thick-bottomed pan and turn the chicken in the butter to brown it evenly. Transfer the bird to a casserole. Melt the remaining butter in another pan and gently stew the carrots and turnips, cut in quarters, in the butter, with the sugar, for 2–3 minutes. Add the peeled whole onions, potatoes and chopped bacon and cook for a further 3 minutes. Turn all the vegetables into the casserole, add the stock and wine, cover and cook at 190°C (375°F)/Gas 5 for 1¼ hours.

42

Chicken Mornay

1.35-kg (3-lb) chicken
500 ml (1 pint) chicken stock
6 peppercorns
1 bayleaf
sprig of rosemary
225 g (8 oz) noodles
25 g (1 oz) butter
25 g (1 oz) plain flour
500 ml (1 pint) milk
salt and pepper
175 g (6 oz) grated cheese
10 ml (2 teaspoons) caraway
  seeds
extra butter

Poach the chicken in the stock with the peppercorns, bayleaf and rosemary for 1¼ hours. Cook the noodles in boiling salted water for 10 minutes, until tender. Melt the butter, stir in the flour and cook gently for 1 minute. Blend in the milk and thicken the sauce over a moderate heat. Season and add the cheese. Drain the noodles and toss them in a little butter with the caraway seeds. Put this on a heatproof serving dish. Place the chicken on top of the noodles and coat it with the sauce. Place it under the grill for a few minutes until it starts to turn golden.

Italian Chicken with Lemon Rice

1.5-kg (3½-lb) chicken
1 clove garlic
2 medium onions
sprig of thyme
sprig of marjoram
salt and pepper
30 ml (2 tablespoons) olive oil
450 g (1 lb) long-grain rice
75 g (3 oz) grated Parmesan
  cheese
1 lemon
2 eggs
5 ml (1 teaspoon) chopped
  marjoram

Put the chicken into cold water to cover with the peeled garlic, 1 onion, herbs and seasonings. Poach for 1½ hours. Take out the chicken and keep it warm. Heat the oil and fry the remaining chopped onion until soft and golden. Stir in the rice and continue stirring over a low heat until the rice has absorbed all the oil. Add salt and pepper and 250 ml (½ pint) chicken stock. Simmer gently and, as the liquid is absorbed, add more chicken stock (in all about 1 litre [2 pints]). When the liquid has been absorbed and the rice is tender, remove it from the heat. Stir in half the cheese with the grated lemon rind and half the juice. Stir in the well-beaten eggs. Put this into a serving dish, sprinkle with the remaining cheese, and serve it with the chicken.

Country Chicken Casserole

1.5-kg (3½-lb) chicken
25 g (1 oz) butter
30 ml (2 tablespoons) cooking
  oil
175 g (6 oz) unsmoked streaky
  bacon
100 g (4 oz) mushrooms
45 ml (3 tablespoons) chicken
  stock
pinch of garlic salt
pepper
1 bayleaf
4 tomatoes

Heat the butter and oil and brown the chicken all over. Put the chicken into a casserole. Chop the bacon and mushrooms and cook them in the fat for 5 minutes, stirring well. Add the stock, garlic salt and pepper and pour this over the chicken. Cover and cook at 180°C (350°F)/Gas 4 for 1 hour. Peel the tomatoes and cut them in slices. Add the tomatoes and bayleaf to the casserole and continue cooking for 30 minutes. White wine or cider may be used instead of stock.

Toscana Chicken

1.5-kg (3½-lb) chicken
1 bayleaf
6 peppercorns
1 cucumber
15 ml (1 tablespoon) chopped
  parsley
50 g (2 oz) butter
salt and pepper
100 g (4 oz) button mushrooms
25 g (1 oz) plain flour
500 ml (1 pint) stock
2 lemons
125 ml (¼ pint) cream

Poach the chicken gently in water with the bayleaf and peppercorns for 1¼ hours. Peel the cucumber and cut it into strips about 2.5 cm (1 in) long, toss it in half the butter until tender, and add the parsley. Season to taste. Toss the halved mushrooms in butter until tender. Melt the remaining butter, stir in the flour and cook for 2 minutes. Blend in the stock and thicken it over a moderate heat. Cut the rind of the lemons into needle-sized shreds and then squeeze the juice from the whole lemons. Add the lemon juice to the sauce. Put the chicken on a serving dish and surround it with the cucumber and mushrooms. Just before serving, add the cream to the sauce and spoon it over the chicken. Sprinkle the lemon shreds down the centre of the bird and serve.

Chicken in Grapefruit Sauce

1.35-kg (3-lb) chicken
50 g (2 oz) butter
15 ml (1 tablespoon) brandy
250 ml (½ pint) giblet stock
75 ml (3 fl oz) dry sherry
salt and pepper
1 grapefruit

Remove the giblets from the bird and simmer them to make stock. Melt the butter and brown the chicken on all sides. Drain off the surplus fat. Pour the brandy over the chicken and light it with a match. When the flames have died down, put the chicken into an ovenware dish, with the stock, cover and cook at 170°C (325°F)/Gas 3 for 1 hour. Strain off the juices and mix them with the sherry, seasoning well. Peel the grapefruit and remove half the segments, taking all skin from them. Squeeze the juice from the remaining grapefruit half and add this to the other liquid. Simmer to reduce this by half. Stir in the whole grapefruit sections and pour the sauce over the chicken.

Greek Chicken with Aubergines

1.5-kg (3¼-lb) chicken
30 ml (2 tablespoons) olive oil
225 g (8 oz) small onions
350 g (12 oz) aubergines
225 g (8 oz) courgettes
100 g (4 oz) canned okra
225 g (8 oz) small tomatoes
salt and pepper
sprig of rosemary
125 ml (¼ pint) chicken stock

Heat the oil in a large frying pan and lightly brown the breast of the chicken. Place it in an ovenware dish. Peel the onions, leaving them whole, and fry them in the oil for about 5 minutes until lightly browned. Cut the aubergines into large cubes. Top and tail the courgettes and cut them into 1.25 cm (½ in) slices. Cut the stems from the okra. Add the vegetables to the pan. Cook for a couple of minutes. Remove the pan from the heat and stir in the whole tomatoes, salt and pepper. Place the vegetables around the chicken, pour over the stock and add the sprig of rosemary. Cover the dish and bake at 190°C (375°F)/Gas 5 for 1½ hours, until tender.

45

Tarragon Chicken

1.35-kg (3-lb) chicken
25 g (1 oz) butter
1 medium onion
2 carrots
30 ml (2 tablespoons) celery
  leaves
4 sprigs of parsley
1 clove
10 ml (2 teaspoons) salt
15 ml (1 tablespoon) tarragon
2 egg yolks

Melt the butter and cook the sliced onion and carrots, with a lid on, for 10 minutes, until soft but not browned. Put them into a casserole with the celery leaves and parsley. Put the chicken on top and pour on 2 pints boiling water. Add the clove, salt and half the tarragon. Cover and cook at 170°C (325°F)/Gas 3 for $1\frac{1}{2}$ hours. Drain off the liquid from the chicken and measure out 500 ml (1 pint). Put this into a saucepan and boil it until reduced to 250 ml ($\frac{1}{2}$ pint). Put the egg yolks into a bowl and stir in a little of the hot liquid. Gradually add the remaining hot stock and the rest of the chopped tarragon. Pour this over the chicken before serving.

5   Barbecues and Spit-roasting

Many families now have outdoor barbecues or oven-spits, and poultry cooked in this way is delicious. These methods do, however, need careful handling to be successful and to avoid producing charred skin containing raw flesh. Plenty of time must always be allowed for cooking (chicken joints take about 45 minutes to cook thoroughly on a barbecue grill), and the poultry must be completely thawed beforehand. Delicious sauces are part of the barbecue scene, and help to keep chicken meat moist and succulent with a crisp and tasty skin.

STARTING THE BARBECUE

A barbecue fire must be lit quickly, and the fuel brought to the correct heat before cooking. Heat has to be maintained, without smoke, sparks and flare-ups, and unpleasant smells from burning food must be prevented. Charcoal burns from the bottom to the top and needs bottom ventilation. Fires should be arranged to take advantage of any prevailing wind, but stiff breezes can be avoided by using a hood or windshield. The charcoal may be started with an ordinary crumbled firelighter, or with an electric or gas firelighter if near the house. Newspaper or twigs will give a slow start and bellows may be needed to get the charcoal glowing well.

When the charcoal is burning evenly, it should be spread out under the grill to cover the whole cooking surface for normal barbecue cooking. For spit cooking, the fire must be piled about 7.5 cm (3 in) deep behind the food on the spit and extending just underneath it.

A barbecue fire has to be lit at least 30 minutes before cooking starts, and additional fuel should be added at the edge of the fire, not on top of the burning charcoal. The heat must be even and flowing, but the charcoal must not be flaming. The fire will look radiant and will appear grey in daylight, but glowing red at night. Food should never be cooked over flames or thick smoke. Cooking time will depend on the heat of the fire, the distance between fire and food, and the temperature of the food when cooking begins. Food is best used at room temperature and should not be taken straight from the refrigerator to the barbecue.

Brush the grill lightly with oil before putting food on it. Put the chicken joints cut side down on the grill first to seal them, then turn them over to cook the skin side. Keep turning and basting, and make sure the chicken is cooked through completely (test with

47

a skewer or sharp knife) so that no pink juices run and the flesh near the bone is not tinged with pink. Use any barbecue sauce to baste the poultry, brushing it on with a small paint brush, and serve any surplus sauce as an accompaniment. Serve barbecued chicken with a crisp green salad and plenty of crusty bread.

Herb Marinade for Chicken

100 g (4 fl oz) oil
50 g (2 fl oz) lemon juice
2.5 ml (½ teaspoon) salt
1.2 ml (¼ teaspoon) pepper
2.5 ml (½ teaspoon) marjoram
2.5 ml (½ teaspoon) thyme
30 ml (2 tablespoons) parsley
1 clove garlic
1 large onion

Mix the oil, lemon juice, salt and pepper. Chop the herbs finely and then chop the garlic and onion. Mix all the ingredients together and pour this over the chicken. Leave the chicken in a cold place for 2–3 hours, before draining, Grill the chicken and baste with the marinade. If liked, 1 teaspoon rosemary may be substituted for the other herbs.

Wine Marinade for Chicken

2 carrots
2 onions
2 cloves garlic
60 ml (4 tablespoons) olive oil
salt and pepper
sprig of thyme
sprig of parsley
1 bayleaf
100 ml (8 fl oz) white wine

Slice the carrots and onions thinly and chop the garlic. Cook them in the oil until lightly browned. Add the salt, pepper and herbs and just cover with water. Simmer for 10 minutes. Add the wine, bring the mixture to the boil, and cool before pouring it over the chicken. Leave in a cold place for 2–3 hours, then drain the chicken. Grill the chicken and baste it with the marinade.

Uncooked Barbecue Sauce

30 ml (2 tablespoons) savoury
    bottled brown sauce
15 ml (1 tablespoon) vinegar
10 ml (2 teaspoons)
    Worcestershire sauce
2.5 ml ($\frac{1}{2}$ teaspoon) made
    mustard
15 ml (1 tablespoon) lemon juice
25 g (1 oz) soft brown sugar

Mix all the ingredients together thoroughly and use this to baste the chicken and to serve as an accompaniment.

Special Barbecue Sauce

50 g (2 oz) butter
1 medium onion
1 clove garlic
30 ml (2 tablespoons) vinegar
200 ml (8 fl oz) water
15 ml (1 tablespoon) made
    mustard
25 g (1 oz) demerara sugar
1 thick slice of lemon
pinch of cayenne pepper
30 ml (2 tablespoons)
    Worcestershire sauce
90 ml (6 tablespoons) tomato
    ketchup
30 ml (2 tablespoons) tomato
    purée
salt and pepper

Melt the butter in a pan and fry the finely chopped onion and crushed garlic for 3 minutes. Stir in the vinegar, water, mustard, sugar, lemon and cayenne pepper. Bring this to the boil and simmer for 15 minutes. Stir in the remaining ingredients, season to taste and continue cooking for 5 minutes. Take out the lemon slice. Use this sauce to baste the poultry, and also serve it as an accompaniment.

Devilled Barbecue Chicken

4 chicken joints
10 ml (2 teaspoons) salt
10 ml (2 teaspoons) sugar
5 ml (1 teaspoon) pepper
5 ml (1 teaspoon) ground ginger
5 ml (1 teaspoon) mustard
    powder
2.5 ml (½ teaspoon) curry
    powder
50 g (2 oz) butter
30 ml (2 tablespoons) tomato
    sauce
15 ml (1 tablespoon) mushroom
    ketchup
15 ml (1 tablespoon)
    Worcestershire sauce
15 ml (1 tablespoon) soy sauce
15 ml (1 tablespoon) plum jam
4 drops Tabasco sauce

Put the chicken joints in a shallow dish. Mix the salt, sugar, pepper, ginger, mustard and curry powder, and cover the chicken thoroughly with the mixture. Leave for 1 hour. Melt the butter and brush it over the chicken joints. Grill them for 10 minutes on each side over a medium heat until brown and crisp. Mix the tomato sauce, mushroom ketchup, Worcestershire sauce, soy sauce, plum jam and Tabasco sauce together with any remaining butter. Heat this gently and use it to baste the chicken frequently until the chicken is completely cooked. Use any remaining sauce as an accompaniment.

Pineapple Chicken

4 chicken joints
100 ml (4 fl oz) oil
5 ml (1 teaspoon) salt
1.2 ml (¼ teaspoon) pepper
225 g (8 oz) canned crushed
    pineapple
175 g (6 oz) soft brown sugar
15 ml (1 tablespoon) lemon juice
15 ml (1 tablespoon) made
    mustard

Brush the chicken joints well with oil and season them with salt and pepper. Grill the joints on both sides until the skin is golden and the meat almost cooked through. Drain the pineapple, reserving the juice. Mix the pineapple, 1 tablespoon reserved juice, sugar, lemon juice, mustard and a pinch of salt. Brush this over both sides of the chicken joints and grll them for 10 minutes more, turning them often and brushing them well with the pineapple glaze. Serve any remaining glaze as a sauce.

50

Charcoal Chicken

1.8-kg (4-lb) chicken
1 clove garlic
120 ml (8 tablespoons) olive oil
125 ml (¼ pint) red wine
salt and pepper
10 ml (2 teaspoons) made
    mustard
1 medium onion
4 drops Tabasco sauce
1 bayleaf
45 ml (3 tablespoons) soy sauce
45 ml (3 tablespoons) tomato
    sauce
90 ml (6 tablespoons) stock

Split the chicken in half lengthwise. Crush the garlic clove and mix it with half the oil, the wine, salt, pepper, mustard, sliced onion, Tabasco sauce, bayleaf, soy sauce and tomato sauce. Pour this over the chicken halves and leave them in a cold place for 6 hours. Drain the chicken and reserve the liquid. Dry the chicken with kitchen paper and then rub the pieces with the remaining oil. Grill them over charcoal until well browned and cooked through.

Put the reserved liquid into a thick-bottomed pan on the barbecue grill and heat it up. Add the grilled chicken and simmer without a lid for 15 minutes. Add the stock and continue cooking for 5 minutes. This dish may of course be cooked using a conventional indoor grill, but the charcoal gives it a special flavour.

Spatchcock Chicken

small roasting chickens
salt and pepper
lemon juice
butter
fine breadcrumbs

Split the birds in half and flatten each half on a board. Skewer each leg flat. Sprinkle the pieces with salt, pepper and lemon juice and leave them in a cool place for 30 minutes. Heat the grill until it is very hot. Brush the chicken halves with melted butter and grill them on each side for 5 minutes, until golden, brushing the pieces with butter during this time. Sprinkle the pieces with crumbs and more butter and cook them under a lower grill until the crumbs are crisp and the chicken tender. Serve with wedges of lemon, and a garnish of watercress. Very small chickens, about the size of poussins, are most suitable for this dish.

Spit-roasting

Many barbecues and ovens are fitted with spits. While this cooking method requires some practice, the results are very worthwhile. The method is particularly suitable for smaller birds up to 1.35 kg (3 lb), and the birds must be very neatly trussed. No wings or flaps of meat should be allowed to hang loose, as they can burn and they also unbalance the spit. When the bird is trussed, an extra couple of loops of string round the body will keep the legs and wings secure.

It is a good idea to put the bird in position and rotate the spit without heat, to see if it is evenly and correctly balanced. Insert the spit rod through the centre of gravity and fix it with spit forks. An imperfectly balanced spit will put the motor under strain and it will wear out quickly. Poultry should be spitted parallel to the backbone, bringing the spit rod between the tail and legs. Cook one bird in the centre of the spit. If small birds are being barbecued, dovetail them on the spit, alternating breast-side up and breast-side down, and push them together tightly. Very small birds can be spitted vertically, alternating heads and tails, running the rod through the lower part of the breasts.

To ensure perfectly cooked meat, use a barbecue thermometer inserted in the thickest part of the meat, between the breast and thigh. Put the thermometer at a slight angle to the spit rod so that it will not fall out as the spit revolves, and make sure it does not touch the fire, drip pan or the hood of the barbecue. The meat is cooked when the marked temperature is recorded on the thermometer. If a special barbecue thermometer is not available, use an unpainted, all-metal thermometer.

On a barbecue, the fire for spit-roasting should be at the back of the grill, with a drip pan at the front to catch the food juices. This prevents fat falling on the fire, causing flare-ups and smoke. Make a pan from heavy duty foil or use a shallow meat pan slightly longer than the bird being cooked. Put the pan a little forward, but under the bird, before starting to run the motor, and be sure that there are no coals or ashes under the drip pan which may cause the pan juices to burn.

The grill should be well heated, and the bird basted with oil or butter before cooking, and then again frequently during cooking. The heat may be lowered once the bird has turned golden. During cooking, the flesh shrinks and the prongs of the forks on either side of the bird may need adjusting to hold it securely. The bird must always be at a constant distance from the fire and just in front of it, so that heat is evenly maintained and all the juices run into the drip pan.

Spit-Roast Chicken with Fruit

1.35-kg (3-lb) chicken
1 cooking apple
25 g (1 oz) seedless raisins
salt
25 g (1 oz) butter
125 ml ($\frac{1}{4}$ pint) chicken stock
60 ml (4 tablespoons) single
  cream
squeeze of lemon juice

Peel, core and dice the apple. Mix it with the raisins and a pinch of salt and fill the body cavity of the chicken. Spread soft butter on the chicken and fix it securely on the spit. Cook until golden, which will take about 1 hour. Mix the juices from the drip pan with the stock, cream and lemon juice. Heat this gently and serve it with the chicken.

Spit-Roast Chicken with Rosemary

1.35-kg (3-lb) chicken
1 chicken liver
sprig of rosemary
50 g (2 oz) butter
salt and pepper
olive oil

Cut the liver in small pieces. Stuff the bird with the liver, rosemary and butter. Sprinkle it well with salt and pepper, and fix it securely on the spit. Brush the bird with olive oil and cook until it is golden, which will take about 1 hour, while basting with the pan juices. Tarragon or thyme may be used instead of rosemary.

6   Chicken Joints

Chicken joints are extremely versatile and it is well worth while keeping a bag of them in the freezer. Fresh joints may also be purchased, or birds cut up by the butcher to order. Joints can be used for single meals for small families, or for full scale entertaining, but the recipes in this chapter are basically designed for 4 people. Quantities of sauce are generous, so that an extra chicken joint can be included for a larger family.

Joints can vary considerably in size. Small chickens may simply be cut in quarters, but with larger birds each section (such as a leg) can be divided to make two joints. Choose the joints to suit your family's appetites, and perhaps use six small pieces rather than four large ones, so that those who eat well may have two portions, while the lighter eaters will be happy with one piece each. If you want to joint a bird yourself, please refer to Chapter One.

If you are using frozen chicken joints, these must be completely thawed before use. They should then be wiped completely dry with kitchen paper, as excess moisture may spoil a dish. Some recipes specify skinned chicken joints, and this is important when a sauce needs to soak into the meat to flavour it. On the other hand, golden skin can enhance the appearance of a dish and may be left on if preferred.

Serve chicken joints, which are cooked in sauce, with pasta, rice, or mashed or boiled potatoes to 'mop up' the sauces, or with crusty bread. Grilled and fried joints are good with crusty bread and vegetables, a salad or watercress. A wedge of lemon to squeeze over the meat will help to reduce some of the richness of joints cooked in fat, and a little chutney will help to offset the somewhat bland flavour of plainly cooked chicken meat.

Curry is particularly good made with chicken joints and a number of curry dishes are included in this chapter. They may be delicate in flavour or very hot, according to taste. The onions in curry dishes should be only just coloured in fat, as any burned pieces will ruin the flavour. These dishes are all made with curry powder which can be easily stored and is always to hand – milk and hot varieties are obtainable, so carefully choose the one which is most likely to be acceptable to the family. The flavour of curry powder is brought out by being cooked for a minute or two in fat with the other ingredients before any liquid is added. Curry sauces should not be thin or runny, so follow the quantities of ingredients carefully. Serve a variety of side dishes with curry, such as rice, poppadums, chutney, sliced bananas, nuts and raisins, cucumber in yoghurt, and desiccated coconut.

Crisp Chicken

4 chicken joints
15 g (½ oz) seasoned flour
50 g (2 oz) butter
30 ml (2 tablespoons) oil
1 clove garlic
1 medium onion
900 g (2 lb) canned tomatoes
200 ml (8 fl oz) dry cider
100 ml (4 fl oz) water
salt and pepper

Topping:
25 g (1 oz) butter
2 rashers bacon
50 g (2 oz) fresh
breadcrumbs
30 ml (2 tablespoons) chopped
  parsley
50 g (2 oz) grated Parmesan
  cheese

Wipe the chicken joints and coat them with the seasoned flour. Heat the butter and oil and cook the chicken until golden brown on all sides. Take it out of the pan and keep it on one side. Add the crushed garlic and finely chopped onion to the fat in the pan and cook it until soft and golden. Add the tomatoes with their liquid, mashing them well so that they break up. Add the cider, water, salt and pepper. Put the chicken into a casserole and pour over the other ingredients. Cover and cook at 180°C (350°F)/Gas 4 for 40 minutes.

Just before serving, make the topping, by tossing the finely chopped bacon and the breadcrumbs in the butter, until the bacon is crisp and the breadcrumbs golden. Add the parsley and cheese and sprinkle this over the chicken.

Golden Fruited Chicken

4 chicken joints
125 ml (¼ pint) rosé wine
30 ml (2 tablespoons) honey
50 g (2 oz) butter
100 g (4 oz) dried apricots

Wipe the chicken joints and put them into a dish with the wine. Leave them in a cold place for 2 hours. Remove the chicken from the wine and dry it thoroughly. Mix the honey and butter together and spread this generously on the chicken pieces, reserving about ¼ of the mixture. Put the apricots into a bowl, pour some boiling water over them and leave them to stand for 10 minutes. Put the wine in the bottom of a casserole and add the drained apricots and the chicken joints. Cover and cook at 180°C (350°F)/Gas 4 for 45 minutes. Take out the chicken pieces and put them, cut side down, on a grilling rack. Brush them with the reserved honey mixture and grill until golden. Serve with the apricot and wine sauce.

Chicken in Cider-Apple Sauce

4 chicken joints
50 g (2 oz) butter
2 cooking apples
1 medium onion
3 sticks celery
15 g (½ oz) plain flour
75 ml (3 fl oz) dry cider
375 ml (¾ pint) water
1 chicken stock cube

Fry the chicken joints in the butter until browned. Put them in a casserole. Fry the sliced onion, celery and apples for 5 minutes, stir in the flour, and add the cider and the stock cube dissolved in water. Cook this to a pulp, then sieve it and pour it over the chicken. Cover and cook at 180°C (350°F)/Gas 4 for one hour. The chicken may be garnished with some apple rings fried in butter.

Chicken with Lemon Barbecue Sauce

4 chicken joints
plain flour
salt and pepper
1 clove garlic
2.5 ml (½ teaspoon) salt
2.5 ml (½ teaspoon) pepper
1 small onion
125 ml (¼ pint) olive oil
125 ml (¼ pint) lemon juice
1.2 ml (¼ teaspoon) thyme

Wipe the chicken and dust it lightly with flour seasoned with salt and pepper. Heat some fat or oil and cook the chicken until golden on all sides. Lower the heat, cover the pan, and cook the chicken gently until tender and well browned. Meanwhile, make the sauce by crushing the garlic and mixing it well with all the other ingredients. Serve the chicken hot, with vegetables and the cold sauce.

Chicken in Sherry Orange Sauce

4 chicken joints
1 bayleaf
4 peppercorns
25 g (1 oz) butter
25 g (1 oz) plain flour
500 ml (1 pint) chicken stock
2 oranges
15 ml (1 tablespoon) sherry
salt and pepper

Poach the chicken gently in the stock, with the bayleaf and peppercorns, for 35 minutes, until tender. Melt the butter and stir in the flour. Cook gently for 1 minute. Blend in the stock and stir it over a low heat until thick and creamy. Grate the rind of the oranges. Squeeze the juice from the oranges and add it to the sauce with the grated orange rind. Add the sherry and season with salt and pepper. Put the chicken joints in a serving dish and pour over the sauce. The chicken may be garnished with orange slices and watercress.

Chicken and Walnut Casserole

4 chicken joints
45 ml (3 tablespoons) oil
50 g (2 oz) walnut halves
1 medium onion
15 g (½ oz) seasoned flour
250 ml (½ oz) seasoned flour
250 ml (½ pint dry cider
500 ml (1 pint) chicken stock
salt and pepper
pinch of marjoram
squeeze of lemon juice
pinch of paprika
1 clove garlic
1 bayleaf
25 g (1 oz) cornflour
75 ml (3 fl oz) single cream

Wipe the chicken joints. Heat the oil and toss the walnuts in it for 3 minutes. Lift out the walnuts and keep them on one side. Chop the onion finely and cook it in the oil until soft and golden. Toss the chicken joints in the seasoned flour and add them to the oil. Cook them until golden brown on all sides. Add the cider, stock, salt, pepper, marjoram, lemon juice, paprika, crushed garlic and bayleaf. Cover and cook gently for 35 minutes. Lift out the chicken and place it on a serving dish. Mix the cornflour with a little water and stir it into the cooking liquid. Bring this to the boil, stirring well. Take out the bayleaf and stir in the walnuts. Cook for 1 minute, then take this off the heat. Stir in the cream and pour it over the chicken. Serve with rice.

Chicken Breasts in Orange Sauce

4 chicken breasts
15 ml (1 tablespoon) oil
50 g (2 oz) butter
salt and pepper

Sauce:
100 ml (4 oz) dry orange wine
1 small onion
pinch of ground mace
1 bayleaf
3 peppercorns
25 g (1 oz) butter
15 g (½ oz) plain flour
375 ml (¾ pint) chicken stock
salt and pepper
100 ml (4 fl oz) milk
30 ml (2 tablespoons) single cream

Start making the sauce before cooking the chicken. Put the orange wine, finely chopped onion, mace, bayleaf and peppercorns into a pan and simmer this until reduced by half. In another pan, melt half the butter, work in the flour and gradually add the chicken stock. Season and stir this over a low heat until the sauce thickens. Strain in the orange wine mixture, bring it to the boil and add the milk. Stir gently over a low heat for 3 minutes. Take off the heat and stir in the cream and remaining butter.

Meanwhile, season the chicken breasts with salt and pepper and fry them in the oil and butter until cooked and golden. Put them on a serving dish and pour over the sauce. The wine may be homemade or bought.

Golden Chicken

4 chicken joints
4 rashers streaky bacon
30 ml (2 tablespoons) oil
15 g (½ oz) butter
25 g (1 oz) caster sugar
15 ml (1 tablespoon) vinegar
125 ml (¼ pint) chicken stock
225 g (8 oz) tomatoes
1 orange
salt and pepper
chopped parsley

Stretch the bacon rashers with the back of a flat-bladed knife and wrap each one round a chicken joint. Heat the oil and butter and fry the chicken joints for 5 minutes until golden brown. Remove the chicken and pour off the fat. Heat the sugar in the pan until golden and then pour in the vinegar and stock. Peel the tomatoes and cut them in thick slices. Add the tomatoes to the pan with the grated rind and juice of the orange and season well with salt and pepper. Put in the chicken joints, cover and simmer for 1 hour. Put the chicken joints on a serving dish. Simmer the pan juices to make a thick glaze. Spoon this over the chicken and sprinkle on some chopped parsley.

Wine Merchant's Chicken

4 chicken joints
75 ml (5 tablespoons) oil
50 g (2 oz) butter
50 g (2 oz) mushrooms
2 shallots (or 1 small onion)
100 g (4 oz) lean bacon
1 clove garlic
25 g (1 oz) flour
salt and pepper
250 ml (½ pint) stock
250 ml (½ pint) red wine

Wipe the chicken joints. Heat the oil in a thick-bottomed pan and brown the chicken. Add a pinch of salt and lower the heat. Put on a lid but leave it slightly aslant so that the chicken pieces are not completely covered and air gets in. Cook for 25 minutes until the chicken is cooked through. Meanwhile, melt the butter and cook the chopped mushrooms, shallots or onions, crushed garlic and chopped ham until golden, stirring well. Stir in the flour and cook it until golden. Add the stock and wine gradually and cook this gently until smooth and creamy. Season to taste. Serve the pieces of chicken with the hot sauce poured over them.

Chicken Fillets in Redcurrant Sauce

6–8 chicken fillets
25 g (1 oz) butter
225 g (8 oz) redcurrant jelly
125 ml (¼ pint) water
50 g (2 oz) redcurrants
10 ml (2 teaspoons) arrowroot
juice of ½ lemon
salt and pepper

Toss the fillets lightly in hot butter for 5 minutes. Mix together the redcurrant jelly, water and redcurrants. Thicken this mixture slightly with arrowroot. Add the redcurrant sauce to the chicken, cover and simmer it gently for 20 minutes, until tender. Add the lemon juice, season to taste and serve with buttered potatoes and a green salad.

Chicken in Port

4 chicken joints
50 g (2 oz) butter
45 ml (3 tablespoons) port
125 ml (¼ pint) stock
2.5 ml (½ teaspoon) marjoram
pinch of ground cinnamon
salt and pepper
1 medium onion
2 cloves
1 bayleaf
225 g (8 oz) button mushrooms

Wipe the chicken joints and then fry them lightly in the butter until just golden. Add the port and stock, marjoram, cinnamon, salt and pepper. Stick the cloves into the onion and add this to the pan with the bayleaf. Cover and simmer for 20 minutes. Add the whole mushrooms and continue cooking for 10 minutes. Remove the onion and bayleaf before serving.

Chicken in Almond Cream Sauce

4 chicken joints
1 lemon
75 g (3 oz) butter
30 ml (2 tablespoons) oil
125 ml (¼ pint) double cream
salt and pepper

Wipe the chicken joints. Cut the lemon in half and squeeze the juice over the chicken. Melt 50 g (2 oz) butter with the oil and fry the chicken pieces slowly until golden brown and tender. Take them out of the pan and keep them hot. Add the remaining butter and fry the blanched and split almonds until golden. Drain off the fat. Add the cream to the pan, season with salt and pepper and heat gently. Pour this over the chicken and garnish it with the remaining lemon, cut in slices.

Drunken Chicken Breasts

4 chicken breasts
salt and pepper
100 g (4 oz) butter
15 g (½ oz) mustard powder
125 ml (¼ pint) tomato sauce
30 ml (2 tablespoons) stock
30 ml (2 tablespoons) dry white
   wine
90 ml (6 tablespoons) brandy
90 ml (6 tablespoons) Madeira

Season the chicken breasts with salt and pepper. Melt $\frac{3}{4}$ of the butter and fry the chicken breasts until golden on all sides. Mix together the remaining butter with the mustard, tomato sauce and stock and add this to the cooking juices. Pour in the wine and continue simmering the chicken breasts for 20 minutes. Just before serving, stir in the brandy and Madeira. Serve with rice.

59

Chicken in Ginger Orange Sauce

4 chicken breasts
100 g (4 oz) butter
25 g (1 oz) plain flour
  2.5 ml (½ teaspoon) salt
1.2 ml (¼ teaspoon) pepper
25 g (1 oz) soft brown sugar
2.5 ml (½ teaspoon) ground
  ginger
200 ml (8 fl oz) orange juice
200 ml (8 fl oz) water
2.5 ml (½ teaspoon) Tabasco
  sauce
1 orange

Sprinkle the chicken with some of the salt and brown it in hot butter. Remove the chicken from the pan. Stir the flour, salt, pepper, brown sugar and ginger into the remaining butter until smooth. Slowly stir in the orange juice, water and Tabasco sauce. Cook and stir until the mixture thickens and comes to the boil. Reduce the heat, add the chicken, cover and simmer for 30 minutes. Without peeling, slice the orange 1.25 cm (½ in) thick and quarter the slices. Add them to the chicken and simmer for 15 minutes, or until the chicken is tender.

Chicken in White Wine

4 chicken breasts
750 ml (1¼ pints) water
2 chicken stock cubes
3 bayleaves
6 peppercorns
15 ml (3 teaspoons) salt

Sauce:
25 g (1 oz) butter
15 ml (1 tablespoon) oil
1 clove garlic
2 medium onions
200 ml (8 fl oz) dry white wine
450 g (1 lb) canned tomatoes
15 ml (1 tablespoon) tomato
  purée
sprig of thyme
5 ml (1 teaspoon) sugar
salt and pepper
100 g (4 oz) button mushrooms

Put the chicken breasts in a pan with the water, stock cubes, bayleaves, peppercorns and salt. Bring this to the boil and simmer gently for 30 minutes until tender. Meanwhile put the oil and butter in a saucepan and heat it until the butter is melted. Add the crushed garlic and finely chopped onions. Cook these until soft and golden and then stir in the wine. Add the drained tomatoes, tomato purée, thyme, sugar, salt and pepper. Stir well, cover and simmer gently for 20 minutes.

Drain the cooked chicken breasts and place them on a warm serving dish. Coat them with the sauce and garnish them with button mushrooms cooked in a little butter. The chicken stock can be used for cooking some long-grain rice to accompany the dish.

Celebration Chicken

6 chicken joints
15 ml (1 tablespoon) oil
5 ml (1 teaspoon) sugar
10 ml (2 teaspoons) tomato
  purée
1 small onion
250 ml (½ pint) mayonnaise
5 ml (1 teaspoon) curry powder
squeeze of lemon juice
30 ml (2 tablespoons) mango
  chutney
125 ml (¼ pint) water

Brush the joints with oil, season and wrap them in tin foil. Cook them at 190°C (375°F)/Gas 5 for approximately 45 minutes, or until the chicken is cooked through and tender. Meanwhile, heat the oil in a saucepan, add the chopped onions and fry them gently until they are soft, but not coloured. Add the curry powder, tomato purée, lemon juice and water. Season, and simmer without a lid for about 15 minutes. Leave this to cool. Push the mango chutney through a sieve and add this purée to the mayonnaise. Mix in the cooled onion mixture and chill. When the chicken has cooked and has been allowed to cool, pour the sauce over each joint and serve it with a crisp green salad.

Chicken in Sherry Cream Sauce

4 chicken joints
plain flour
salt and pepper
75 g (3 oz) butter
1 medium onion
200 ml (8 fl oz) dry white wine
200 ml (8 fl oz) stock
few drops of mushroom ketchup
bayleaf
sprig of parsley
sprig of thyme

Sauce:
25 g (1 oz) butter
15 g (½ oz) plain flour
200 ml (8 fl oz) double cream
15 ml (1 tablespoon) sherry
5 ml (1 teaspoon) brandy

Coat the chicken pieces lightly in flour seasoned with salt and pepper. Melt the butter and cook the chicken pieces with the minced onion for 20 minutes. Cover the pan so that the chicken remains pale and does not brown. Add the wine, stock, mushroom ketchup and herbs and continue simmering for 15 minutes, until the chicken is tender. Drain the chicken and keep it hot. In a clean pan, melt the butter for the sauce and work in the flour. Cook for 1 minute and strain in the cooking liquid. Simmer for 10 minutes until smooth and creamy. Stir in the cream, sherry and brandy and reheat. Pour this over the chicken and serve it hot.

Dijon Chicken

4 chicken joints
50 g (2 oz) butter
500 ml (1 pint) dry white wine
1.2 ml (¼ teaspoon) tarragon
sprig of thyme
1 bayleaf
2.5 ml (½ teaspoon) salt
1.2 ml (¼ teaspoon) pepper
2 egg yolks
30 ml (2 tablespoons) French
  mustard
30 ml (2 tablespoons)
  commercial soured cream

Wipe the chicken joints and cook them in butter until well browned on both sides. Add the wine, tarragon, thyme, bayleaf, salt and pepper and bring this to the boil. Put the chicken and liquid into a casserole and cook for 40 minutes at 170°C (325°F)/Gas 3. Beat the egg yolks lightly in a bowl, and gradually pour in the sauce from the chicken. Stir in the mustard and soured cream and heat gently, without boiling. Pour this sauce over the chicken before serving.

Slimmer's Spicy Chicken

15 ml (½ oz) butter
1 small onion
30 ml (2 tablespoons)
  Worcestershire sauce
5 ml (1 teaspoon) tomato purée
1 orange
salt and pepper
4 chicken joints

Melt the butter in a pan and cook the finely chopped onion gently for 5 minutes. Pare thin strips of peel from half the orange with a potato peeler and cut these into 'matchsticks'. Finely grate the remaining orange rind and squeeze the juice from the orange. Add the Worcestershire sauce, tomato purée, orange strips, rind and juice to the onion, bring this to the boil and season to taste. Place the chicken joints on large piece of foil in a roasting pan and spoon over the orange baste. Enclose this completely in foil and bake at 200°C (400°F)/Gas 6, for 30 minutes. Uncover the pan and bake for a further 15 minutes until golden brown. To serve, spoon the juices from the roasting pan over the chicken, and serve hot or cold with watercress or a green salad.

Devon Chicken

30 ml (2 tablespoons) oil
25 g (1 oz) butter
4 chicken joints
225 g (8 oz) carrots
1 medium onion
2 sticks celery
25 g (1 oz) plain flour
375 ml ($\frac{3}{4}$ pint) dry cider
salt and pepper
30 ml (2 tablespoons)
   Worcestershire sauce
100 g (4 oz) frozen peas

Heat the oil and butter in a frying pan, and add the chicken joints. Fry them quickly until browned, turning once. Remove the joints from the pan and put them in a casserole. Add the sliced vegetables and fry for 5 minutes. Blend in the flour and cook for 1 minute. Add the cider and Worcestershire sauce and bring it to boiling point, stirring well. Pour the vegetable mixture over the chicken. Cover and cook at 180°C (350°F)/Gas 4 for 1 hour. Add the peas and cook for 10 minutes. Check the seasoning before serving.

Chicken Florentine

450 g (1 lb) spinach
50 g (2 oz) butter
salt and pepper
2 thick slices cooked ham
4 chicken breasts
500 ml (1 pint) cheese sauce

Wash the spinach well and drain it thoroughly. Put it into a pan with the butter, but no water. Cover and cook until the spinach is tender. Drain and chop the spinach, and put it into an ovenware dish. Cut the ham in strips and sprinkle them on the spinach. Skin the chicken breasts and put them on top. Pour on the cheese sauce which should be strongly flavoured and well seasoned. Bake at 180°C (350°F)/Gas 4 for 1 hour, until golden brown.

Stoved Chicken

2 large onions
900 g (2 lb) potatoes
4 chicken joints
50 g (2 oz) butter
salt and pepper
500 ml (1 pint) chicken stock

Slice the onions and cut the potatoes in medium-thick pieces. Brown the chicken joints in half the butter. Put a thick layer of potatoes in a casserole, then a layer of onions and then the chicken joints. Season well with salt and pepper and dot with the remaining butter. Top with another layer of potatoes, then onions and, finally, potatoes. Season with salt and pepper and pour in the stock. Put a piece of buttered greaseproof paper on the top and then a lid. Cook at 150°C (300°F)/Gas 2 for $2\frac{1}{2}$ hours.

Country Casserole

1.35-kg (3-lb) chicken
25 g (1 oz) butter
15 ml (1 tablespoon) oil
225 g (8 oz) potatoes
100 g (4 oz) mushrooms
1 small onion
250 ml (½ pint) stock
15 ml (1 tablespoon) tomato
  purée
5 ml (1 teaspoon) chopped
  mixed herbs
salt and pepper

Joint the chicken into 8 pieces, making sure there is a good portion of breast with each wing joint. Skin the pieces and then cook them in the oil and butter until they are golden on all sides. Drain the chicken and put it into a casserole. Peel the potatoes and slice them thinly. Slice the mushrooms and chop the onions, and fry them for 2 minutes in the fat. Stir in the stock, tomato purée and herbs, and bring this to the boil. Boil for 4 minutes and then pour the sauce over the chicken. Arrange overlapping slices of potato all over the top of the chicken and brush them with a little oil or melted butter. Sprinkle with salt and pepper. Cover and cook at 180°C (350°F)/Gas 4 for 30 minutes. Remove the lid and continue cooking for 30 minutes.

Minty Chicken Surprise

4 chicken joints
25 g (1 oz) melted butter

Stuffing:
1 onion
50 g (2 oz) butter
100 g (4 oz) fresh white
  breadcrumbs
1 lemon
30 ml (2 tablespoons) chopped
  parsley
5 ml (1 teaspoon)
  concentrated mint sauce or
  fresh chopped mint
salt and pepper

Cook the chopped onion in the butter for 5 minutes until soft. Remove from the heat and mix in the other stuffing ingredients. To stuff the chicken, gently lift the skin from as much of the chicken joint as possible and fill this pocket with stuffing. Secure the skin with wooden cocktail sticks. Place the joints in a baking tin and brush them with melted butter. Cook at 200°C (400°F)/Gas 6 for 45 minutes until the chicken is golden brown. Serve with gravy made from the pan juices.

Coq-Au-Vin

6 chicken joints
100 g (4 oz) bacon
100 g (4 oz) small onions or
  shallots
100 g (4 oz) butter
50 g (2 oz) seasoned flour
60 ml (4 tablespoons) brandy
2 cloves garlic
½ bottle red wine
250 ml (½ pint) chicken stock
bayleaf
sprig of parsley
sprig of thyme
100 g (4 oz) button mushrooms
triangles of fried bread
chopped parsley

This casserole method of preparing a classic recipe gives excellent results and is convenient for the cook-hostess. Chop the bacon and onions (if shallots, leave whole). Fry them in half the butter till golden brown. Remove them from the fat and place them in a casserole. Toss the chicken in seasoned flour and fry it in the fat used for the bacon and onions till light brown on all sides. Pour the brandy over the chicken and set light to it. Shake the pan and rotate it until the flames die down. Add the red wine and stock, herbs, crushed garlic, and further seasoning to taste. Put the chicken into the casserole with the onions and bacon and cover it. Cook at 180°C (350°F)/Gas 4 for about 45 minutes, or until the chicken is tender. Remove the casserole from the oven and add the whole mushrooms. Return the dish to oven for 10 minutes.

Meanwhile, melt the remaining butter and blend in the rest of the seasoned flour. Take the casserole from the oven and remove the herbs. Strain off some of the liquid and slowly stir this into the butter and the remaining flour. Pour this back into the casserole, stir until evenly mixed and return to the oven for 5 minutes. Garnish with triangles of fried bread and chopped parsley.

Grilled Chicken with Tarragon

4 chicken joints
6 sprigs fresh tarragon
juice of 1 lemon
15 ml (1 tablespoon) olive oil
pepper
50 g (2 oz) butter

Chop the tarragon and reserve a little for garnishing the dish. Put the chicken joints into a dish and pour on the lemon juice and oil. Sprinkle on the tarragon and a little pepper. Leave the chicken for 1 hour, turning it two or three times. Melt the butter. Drain the chicken and put it into a grill pan. Pour on the melted butter and grill the chicken under a medium heat. Baste it with the marinade during cooking, and turn the chicken once. Cook until the chicken joints are golden and crisp. Serve sprinkled with reserved tarragon and the pan juices.

Chicken Kiev

4 chicken breasts
100 g (4 oz) butter
15 ml (1 tablespoon) chopped
  parsley
15 ml (1 tablespoon) chopped
  chives
1 clove garlic
2.5 ml (½ teaspoon) salt
2.5 ml (½ teaspoon) pepper
50 g (2 oz) plain flour
2 eggs
175 g (6 oz) dry breadcrumbs

Put the chicken breasts between sheets of greaseproof paper and pound them flat with a steak bat or other heavy object. Cream the butter and beat in the herbs, crushed garlic, salt and pepper. Divide this into four pieces and form them into ovals. Chill these until very firm in the refrigerator. Put a piece of butter in the centre of each flattened chicken breast and fold the flesh over to form an envelope. Dip these into the flour, then beaten egg, and then breadcrumbs, to give a really thick layer of crumbs. Chill for 1 hour. Deep-fry in hot oil until golden brown. Drain the chicken on absorbent kitchen paper and serve it hot. These chicken delicacies tend to 'spurt' when cut into, so guests should be warned, or each little parcel carefully cut with a sharp-pointed knife as it is served.

Fried Chicken in a Basket

4 chicken drumsticks
seasoned flour
1 egg
20 ml (4 teaspoons) Dijon
  mustard
175 g (6 oz) fresh breadcrumbs
50 g (2 oz) grated cheese
deep fat for frying
watercress to garnish

Toss the drumsticks in seasoned flour, shaking off any surplus. Blend the mustard with the beaten egg. Mix the breadcrumbs and cheese and make a bed of the mixture on a sheet of greaseproof paper. Take each joint and brush it over carefully with egg and mustard. Place it on the bed of crumbs and cheese and, by tipping the paper, roll each joint in crumbs until completely coated. Press the crumbs on firmly and shake off any surplus. Leave the coating to harden before frying the chicken in deep fat at 190°C (375°F)/Gas 5 for 8–10 minutes, until golden. Drain on soft paper, cover the protruding bone-ends with cutlet frills and arrange the pieces on a napkin in a basket or dish, garnished with watercress. Serve hot with barbecue or tomato sauce and baked jacket potatoes, or cold with tartare sauce and salad.

Cold Spicy Chicken

4 chicken joints
125 ml (¼ pint) chicken stock
5 ml (1 teaspoon) turmeric
5 ml (1 teaspoon) curry powder
5 ml (1 teaspoon) ground ginger
5 ml (1 teaspoon) mustard
    powder
2.5 ml (½ teaspoon) pepper
2.5 ml (½ teaspoon) mixed herbs
1.2 ml (¼ teaspoon) ground
    mixed spice
25 g (1 oz) butter

Poach the joints in the stock until tender. Mix together the herbs and spices and sprinkle this over the drained and dried joints of chicken. Leave them for 30 minutes. Then brush the joints with melted butter and put them under a medium grill until they turn golden brown and crisp. Leave them to cool. Serve with mango chutney and salad.

Mustard Chicken

4 chicken joints
75 g (3 oz) butter
30 ml (2 tablespoons) oil
salt and pepper
15 ml (1 tablespoon) made
    English mustard
60 ml (4 tablespoons) French
    mustard
3 spring onions
2.5 ml (½ teaspoon) thyme
175 g (6 oz) dried breadcrumbs

Wipe the chicken pieces and brush them with melted butter and oil. Place them, skin side down, in a grill pan and cook them under a medium grill for 10 minutes each side, basting two or three times, and sprinkling them with salt and pepper. Mix the mustards with the finely chopped onions, thyme and half the remaining fat, to make a thick cream. Brush the chicken with this mixture and then coat the pieces thickly with breadcrumbs. Place the chicken pieces on a rack in the grill pan and pour half the remaining fat over them. Grill under a moderate heat for 5 minutes, then turn and baste with the remaining fat. Continue grilling until the chicken is golden brown. Serve hot or cold.

Kentucky-Fried Chicken

4 chicken joints
plain flour
salt and pepper
oil for frying

Wipe the chicken joints very dry and toss them in plenty of flour, seasoned very well with salt and pepper. Put cooking oil into a deep frying pan (use corn or vegetable oil, not olive oil) to a depth of 3.75 cm (1½ in). Heat the oil until very hot and put in the chicken joints, skin side up. Turn only once during frying. The chicken is cooked when the crust is a rich golden colour. Drain the pieces on absorbent kitchen paper and serve hot or cold.

Picnic Chicken

4 chicken joints
75 g (3 oz) butter
50 g (2 oz) plain flour
5 ml (1 teaspoon) tarragon
5 ml (1 teaspoon) rosemary
1 clove garlic
salt and pepper
1 egg
30 ml (2 tablespoons) milk

Pre-heat the oven to 190°C (375°F)/Gas 5. Put the butter into a shallow baking tin and heat it in the oven until the butter is frothy, but not discoloured. Thoroughly mix together the flour, seasoning, garlic and herbs. Whisk the egg into the milk. Dip the chicken into the egg mixture, then in seasoned flour, and place it in the prepared tin. Spoon the butter over it and cook it for about 45 minutes, turning it over frequently. The chicken is good hot, but is even better served cold.

Quick Chicken Casserole

4 chicken joints
45 ml (3 tablespoons) oil
1 can condensed mushroom soup
125 ml (¼ pint) milk
15 ml (1 tablespoon) chopped
   parsley

Wipe the chicken joints. Heat the oil and cook the chicken over a low heat for 15 minutes, until golden. Drain the chicken and put it into a casserole. Heat the soup and milk until just boiling and pour it over the chicken pieces. Cover and cook at 180°C (350°F)/Gas 4 for 40 minutes. Sprinkle them with chopped parsley. To make this dish more substantial, a packet of mixed frozen vegetables may be added with the soup.

Chicken with Sauce Delilah

4 chicken joints
1 small onion
2 cloves garlic
30 ml (2 tablespoons) lemon
   juice
30 ml (2 tablespoons) soy sauce
salt and pepper
3 drops Tabasco sauce
5 ml (1 teaspoon) ground
   coriander
25 g (1 oz) brown sugar
30 ml (2 tablespoons) apricot
   jam
30 ml (2 tablespoons) salad oil

Make slashes in the chicken joints in two or three places and then put them into a shallow, ovenware dish. Mix all the other ingredients together, pour them over the chicken and leave it for 2 hours, turning occasionally. Bake at 180°C (350°F)/Gas 4 for 25–30 minutes, basting every now and again with the sauce. Serve with jacket potatoes filled with butter mixed with a little sour cream or with cream cheese beaten with a little lemon juice and butter.

Chicken Pilaff St Hubert

4 chicken joints
50 g (2 oz) butter
200 ml (8 fl oz) red wine or
  cider
15 ml (1 tablespoon) redcurrant
  jelly
25 g (1 oz) almonds or cashew
  nuts

Pilaff:
225 g (8 oz) long-grain rice
1 medium onion
40 g (1½ oz) butter
625 ml (1¼ pints) chicken stock
salt and pepper
3 dried apple rings
50 g (2 oz) dried apricots
50 g (2 oz) currants

Soak the apple rings and apricots overnight. Spread the chicken portions with the butter and put them in a roasting tin. Pour over them half the wine or cider. Roast at 180°C (350°F)/Gas 4 for 35 minutes raising the heat to 200°C (400°F)/Gas 6 for the last 5 minutes, to brown thoroughly.

Meanwhile, prepare the pilaff. Soak the currants in hot water for 30 minutes. Using a flameproof casserole, toss the finely chopped onion in half the butter until just coloured. Add the rice and stir well. Add 500 ml (1 pint) stock, season and bring this to the boil. Cover the casserole and put it in the oven under the chicken dish for 12 minutes, or until barely cooked.

While the rice is cooking, stew the apricots and apples for 10 minutes in the water in which they have been soaked. Drain and cut them into pieces. Drain the currants. Stir the fruit carefully into the rice with a fork. If necessary, moisten this with a little stock. Season well and dot the rice with the remaining butter. Cover this with foil and a lid and replace it in the oven. Leave it for 15–20 minutes, forking the rice over once or twice. When the rice is dry, remove it from the oven. Remove the chicken and make up the gravy in the pan, using the remaining wine and some of the stock. Add the redcurrant jelly and boil this thoroughly. Fry the nuts in a little butter until brown. Place the chicken joints on the rice and spoon a little sauce over each piece, serving the remainder in a sauce-boat. Scatter the nuts over the chicken and serve hot.

Portuguese Chicken

4 chicken joints
25 g (1 oz) butter
225 g (8 oz) small onions
2 cloves garlic
1 bayleaf
1 strip lemon peel
100 g (4 oz) long-grain rice
salt and pepper
250 ml ($\frac{1}{2}$ pint) white wine

Wipe the chicken joints and smear the butter over them. Put them into a deep casserole and surround them with peeled onions and crushed garlic. Add the bayleaf and lemon peel. Sprinkle in the rice, season well and pour in the wine. Cover this with a piece of foil and a lid. Cook at 150°C (300°F)/Gas 2 for $2\frac{1}{2}$ hours. Serve with a green salad.

Algerian Chili Chicken

1.35-kg (3-lb) chicken
2 fresh chillies
30 ml (2 tablespoons) thick
  honey
1 egg
pinch of curry powder
juice of $\frac{1}{4}$ lemon
10 ml (2 teaspoons) sage
125 ml ($\frac{1}{4}$ pint) olive oil
pinch of salt

Split the chicken in half lengthways. Loosen the skin over the breast, but do not remove it. Mix together the honey, egg yolk, curry powder and lemon juice and add the stiffly whipped egg white. Put half this mixture under the skin of each chicken half, and also put one chilli in each side. Rub the skin with the sage, oil and salt. Put the chicken under a hot grill and brown it on each side. Allow a total of 25 minutes' cooking time and keep basting with the oil and the pan juices. Serve with rice.

Chicken Provençale

4 chicken joints
30 ml (2 tablespoons) oil
salt and pepper
1.2 ml ($\frac{1}{4}$ teaspoon) basil
1 clove garlic
1 medium onion
100 g (4 oz) button mushrooms
225 g (8 oz) canned tomatoes
125 ml ($\frac{1}{4}$ pint) dry white wine
125 ml ($\frac{1}{4}$ pint) chicken stock
50 g (2 oz) stuffed olives
pinch of sugar
15 g ($\frac{1}{2}$ oz) cornflour

Heat the oil and fry the chicken portions until browned on all sides. Sprinkle with salt, pepper and basil. Add the crushed garlic, chopped onion, mushrooms, tomatoes, wine and stock. Cover and simmer for 35 minutes. Lift out the chicken, place it on a serving dish and keep it warm. Stir the olives into the sauce and cook for 2–3 minutes to allow them to heat through. Check the seasoning, adding a pinch of sugar, and thicken the sauce with the cornflour blended with a little water. Spoon this over the chicken.

70

Algerian Grilled Chicken

1.35-kg (3-lb) chicken
5 ml (1 teaspoon) salt
50 g (2 oz) butter
90 ml (6 tablespoons) oil
15 g (½ oz) ground almonds
25 g (1 oz) raisins
30 ml (2 tablespoons) lemon
   juice
pinch of Cayenne pepper
5 ml (1 teaspoon) curry powder
pinch of thyme
pinch of turmeric
pinch of ground allspice
15 ml (1 tablespoon) chopped
   fresh herbs (including mint)

If possible, preparations for this dish should be made the day before. Cream the butter until it is soft and mix it with the oil, almonds, raisins, lemon juice, Cayenne pepper, curry powder, thyme, turmeric powder, allspice and herbs (a little mint should be included in the herbs). Leave this mixture overnight so that the flavours blend together. Next day, split the chicken in half, or cut it into quarters. Rub the salt into it and then $\frac{2}{3}$ of the butter mixture. Put the pieces into an oiled grill pan and grill them on all sides under a hot grill until golden. Reduce the grill to a medium heat and cook the chicken for about 25 minutes, turning the pieces often, and rubbing in the remaining mixture until the meat is cooked through. Serve with rice and a tomato or cucumber salad.

Sweet and Sour Chicken

4 chicken joints
30 ml (2 tablespoons) soy sauce
15 ml (1 tablespoon) wine
   vinegar
10 ml (2 teaspoons)
   Worcestershire sauce
15 ml (1 tablespoon) cornflour
225 g (8 oz) canned pineapple
   cubes
225 g (8 oz) ham
half a cucumber
4 sticks celery
2 tomatoes
salt and pepper

Fry the chicken joints in deep fat until golden and tender. Meanwhile, blend together the soy sauce, vinegar, Worcestershire sauce and cornflour. Heat the pineapple juice, made up to 500 ml (1 pint) with water. Pour this over the cornflour mixture and stir until smooth. Return it to the pan and bring it to the boil, stirring until it thickens. Cut the ham into cubes and add it with the drained pineapple. Cut the cucumber and celery into thin strips. Peel the tomatoes, remove the pips and cut the flesh into thin strips. Add the cucumber, celery and tomatoes and season with salt and pepper. Simmer gently for 15 minutes. Add the chicken joints and serve with rice.

Chicken and Saffron Bake

6 chicken joints
45 ml (3 tablespoons) oil
1 medium onion
100 g (4 oz) long-grain rice
225 g (8 oz) canned tomatoes
2.5 ml (½ teaspoon) marjoram
pinch of saffron
250 ml (½ pint) chicken stock
salt and pepper
100 g (4 oz) frozen peas

Heat the oil in a frying pan and put in the seasoned chicken joints. Fry them until lightly browned all over. Remove the joints from the pan and add the chopped onion. Soften this slightly in the remaining oil for 3 minutes and then add the rice and brown lightly. Add the tomatoes, with their juice, and the chicken stock, marjoram and saffron, bring this to the boil and season it well. Pour the rice mixture into a casserole and top it with the chicken joints. Cover and cook at 190°C (375°F)/Gas 5 for 50 minutes. Add the peas to the dish and return it to the oven for 15 minutes.

Chicken with Sesame Seeds

75 g (3 oz) plain flour
salt and pepper
15 ml (1 tablespoon) sesame
    seeds
2.5 ml (½ teaspoon) ground
    coriander
1.2 ml (¼ teaspoon) ground
    ginger
pinch of chilli powder
4 chicken breasts
75 g (3 oz) butter
15 ml (1 tablespoon) olive oil
250 ml (½ pint) chicken stock
45 ml (3 tablespoons) dry white
    wine
15 ml (1 tablespoon) chopped
    parsley
15 ml (1 tablespoon) chopped
    watercress
2 sprigs rosemary
125 ml (¼ pint) double cream
175 ml (6 oz) long-grain rice
25 g (1 oz) melted butter

Season the flour with the salt, pepper, sesame seeds, coriander, ginger and chilli powder. Coat the chicken portions evenly. Fry the chicken in the butter and olive oil for 10 minutes on each side. Transfer the chicken to a warm dish and keep it hot. Stir the remaining seasoned flour into the frying pan and add the chicken stock, rosemary leaves and wine. Bring to the boil and simmer gently for 20 minutes, or until reduced by half. Add the chopped parsley and watercress to the sauce. Stir in the cream and reheat gently. Cook the rice in boiling salted water for 12 minutes. Drain and rinse it with hot water. Stir in the melted butter. Pile the rice into a serving dish and arrange the chicken portions on top. Serve the sauce in a sauce-boat.

Bangkok Chicken

2 chicken breasts
50 g (2 oz) lard
1 medium onion
30 ml (2 tablespoons) preserved
  ginger
75 g (3 oz) button mushrooms
1 clove garlic
pinch of coriander seeds
pinch of salt
pinch of Cayenne pepper
juice of 1 lemon
5 ml (1 teaspoon) Demerara
  sugar
15 ml (1 tablespoon) soy sauce
15 ml (1 tablespoon) vinegar

Cut the chicken breasts into matchstick pieces and brown them lightly in the hot lard. Add the finely chopped onion, chopped ginger, thinly-sliced mushrooms and crushed coriander. Stir well until golden brown. Season with salt and Cayenne pepper. Cover the pan, reduce the heat and leave it to cook for 5 minutes only. Mix together the lemon juice, sugar, soy sauce and vinegar. Stir this into the chicken, bring it to the boil, and serve at once with boiled rice.

Chicken Creaole

4 chicken joints
50 g (2 oz) lard
5 large tomatoes
2 medium onions
1 clove garlic
1 bayleaf
pinch of mixed herbs
15 ml (1 tablespoon) tomato
  sauce
15 g (½ oz) plain flour
30 ml (2 tablespoons) chilli
  sauce
pinch of chilli powder
30 ml (2 tablespoons) chopped
  parsley

Wipe the chicken joints and brown them on all sides in the lard. Lift them out. Peel the tomatoes and add them to the fat with the sliced onions, crushed garlic, bayleaf and mixed herbs. Stir well, until golden brown. Add the tomato sauce and flour and mix thoroughly. Sprinkle a little salt on the chicken pieces and put them into the tomato mixture. Cover and simmer for 30 minutes, stirring occasionally. Just before serving, lift out the chicken and put it on a serving dish. Stir the chilli sauce, chilli powder and parsley into the sauce and add a little more salt and pepper if liked. Pour this over the chicken and serve with plain boiled rice.

Oriental Stuffed Chicken Legs

4 large chicken legs
2 small, boiled potatoes
1 hard-boiled egg
50 g (2 oz) blanched almonds
25 g (1 oz) raisins
1.2 ml (¼ teaspoon) sage
15 ml (1 tablespoon) lemon juice
50 g (2 oz) plain flour
pinch of pepper
pinch of paprika
5 ml (1 teaspoon) salt

Dice the potatoes and egg very finely. Combine these with the sliced almonds, raisins and sage. Sprinkle the mixture with lemon juice and toss it lightly. Make a slit in the thickest part of the chicken legs and fill each with stuffing. Coat the chicken evenly in flour seasoned with pepper, paprika and salt. Place it on a rack to dry slightly. Melt the cooking oil in a heavy frying pan and, when hot, add the chicken and brown it on all sides (about 15 minutes). Reduce the heat, add a little water, cover the pan tightly and continue cooking, turning the pieces occasionally, until tender – about 25 minutes. Remove the lid for the last 5–10 minutes of cooking, to allow the skin to crisp.

Spanish Chicken in Pepper Sauce

8 small chicken joints
salt and pepper
45 ml (3 tablespoons) olive oil
2 large onions
2 cloves garlic
2 small green peppers
2 small red peppers
50 g (2 oz) raw smoked ham
450 g (1 lb) canned tomatoes
8 stoned green olives
8 stoned black olives

Season each chicken joint with a little salt and freshly ground black pepper. Heat the oil in a flameproof casserole and fry the chicken pieces on each side until lightly browned – about 5 minutes. Remove the chicken joints and place them on one side.

Peel and roughly chop the onions and crush the garlic. Cut the pepper into strips. If using tinned red peppers, drain them well on kitchen paper and slice them in the same way. Fry the vegetables in the oil to soften them slightly, but do not let them brown. Stir in the chopped ham and tomatoes and, over a high heat, cook this gently to reduce the liquid in the pan to a fairly thick sauce. Return the chicken pieces to the pan, cover it, and simmer gently for 25 minutes. Stir in the halved olives and check the seasoning. Serve the chicken with saffron rice.

Spanish Chicken

4–6 chicken joints
salt
45 ml (3 tablespoons) oil
1 clove garlic
1 green pepper
450 g (1 lb) canned tomatoes
75 ml (3 fl oz) sherry
1.2 ml ($\frac{1}{4}$ teaspoon) pepper
2.5 ml ($\frac{1}{2}$ teaspoon) paprika
2 whole cloves
1 bayleaf
200 ml (8 fl oz) water
3 courgettes
1 large aubergine

Season the chicken with salt and brown it in the oil. Add the chopped onion, crushed garlic and chopped green pepper and cook for 5 minutes. Add the remaining ingredients, except the courgettes and aubergine, cover and simmer for 30 minutes. Add the sliced courgettes and cubed aubergine and cover and simmer for 15 minutes, or until chicken is tender. Serve with rice.

Cinnamon Chicken

4 chicken joints
30 ml (2 tablespoons) olive oil
1 medium onion
1 medium carrot
1 garlic clove
125 ml ($\frac{1}{4}$ pint) dry white wine
375 ml ($\frac{3}{4}$ pint) chicken stock
2.5 ml ($\frac{1}{2}$ teaspoon) ground cinnamon
salt and pepper
25 g (1 oz) butter
25 g (1 oz) plain flour

Brown the chicken joints on all sides in the oil. Add the chopped onion and carrot and the crushed garlic, and cook for 2 minutes. Drain off excess oil. Add the wine, stock, cinnamon, salt and pepper, cover and simmer for 45 minutes. Remove the chicken and keep it hot.

Melt the butter and work in the flour. Cook for 1 minute and gradually add the cooking liquid. Stir and cook over low heat until the sauce is creamy. Pour over the chicken. Serve with rice.

Swiss Chicken

6 chicken joints
15 ml (1 tablespoon) oil
75 g (3 oz) butter
25 g (1 oz) plain flour
375 ml (¾ pint) milk
125 ml (¼ pint) single cream
50 g (2 oz) Gruyère cheese,
    grated
50 g (2 oz) Parmesan cheese,
    grated
salt and pepper
2 egg yolks

Garnish:
25 g (1 oz) Parmesan cheese,
    grated
15 g (½ oz) butter

Put the oil into a frying pan with 50 g (2 oz) butter. Brown the chicken in the hot fat on all sides until golden. Reduce the heat and continue cooking until the chicken is cooked through which will take about 25 minutes. Melt the remaining butter in a saucepan and stir in the flour. Cook for 1 minute and then stir in the milk. Stir and cook over low heat for 5 minutes. Take off the heat and stir in the grated cheese and cream. Heat very gently to melt the cheese. Remove from the heat and season to taste. Beat in the egg yolks.

Put half this sauce into an ovenware dish and arrange the chicken pieces on top. Cover with the remaining sauce. Sprinkle with the Parmesan cheese and dot with flakes of butter. Cover with foil and cook at 170°C (325°F) Gas 3 for 10 minutes. Remove the foil and continue cooking for 5 minutes to brown the top.

Highland Chicken

4 chicken joints
75 g (3 oz) softened butter
15 ml (1 tablespoon) French
    mustard
juice of ½ lemon
salt and pepper
60 ml (4 tablespoons) whisky
125 ml (¼ pint) single cream

Reserve one-third of the butter, and mix the remainder with the mustard, lemon juice, salt and pepper. Spread this all over the chicken pieces. Heat the remaining butter in a thick pan and brown the chicken pieces all over on a gentle heat. Put on a lid and cook very gently for 30 minutes until the chicken is cooked through.

Pour the whisky over the chicken and let it warm through for a minute. Light the whisky. When the flame has died down, pour in the cream and heat very gently, without boiling, for 5 minutes. Serve with new potatoes.

76

Turkish Honey Chicken

4 chicken joints
50 g (2 oz) butter
10 ml (2 teaspoons) clear honey
salt and pepper
pinch of marjoram
2 oranges

Wipe the chicken joints. Remove the rack from the grill pan and put the butter in the pan. Add the honey, salt, pepper and marjoram. Grate the rind of the oranges into the pan. Remove the skin and pith from the oranges, using a sharp knife. Cut away the pithy membranes and cut the flesh into segments. Keep the segments on one side for decoration. Squeeze any juice from the remaining membranes into the grill pan. Under a gentle heat, melt the butter and honey, then put the chicken joints into the pan and coat them well in the butter mixture. Cook gently, turning them often to cook them evenly, and coat them well each time in the butter mixture, for about 30 minutes. When the chicken is cooked and a glossy golden brown, place it on a serving dish and decorate each piece with orange segments. Serve the sauce, which remains in the grill pan, in a sauce-boat.

Yugoslavian Chicken with Egg Sauce

4 chicken joints
salt and pepper
25 g (1 oz) flour
30 ml (2 tablespoons) olive oil
1 litre (2 pints) milk
1 clove garlic
250 ml (½ pint) chicken stock
3 eggs
30 ml (2 tablespoons) lemon
    juice
pinch of paprika

Place the chicken joints in a saucepan and cover them with cold water. Season with salt and pepper, bring this to the boil and simmer gently for about 30 minutes, until the chicken is tender. Drain the chicken and put it on a deep serving dish. Cover and keep it warm.

Meanwhile, make the sauce. Blend the flour and oil together in a saucepan, and then gradually blend in the milk. Add the crushed garlic clove. Bring this to the boil, stirring all the time, and cook it for a minute. Take the pan off the heat and stir in the chicken stock. Beat the eggs together lightly in a bowl, and then gradually add the lemon juice. Beat the hot liquid, a little at a time, into the eggs. It must be added slowly or the mixture will curdle. Return the sauce to the pan and heat it gently, but do not boil it. Season with salt and pepper to taste. To serve, pour the sauce over the chicken quarters. Sprinkle a little paprika over this and serve it with a salad.

Chicken Cacciatore

4 chicken joints
salt and pepper
30 ml (2 tablespoons) oil
1 small onion
1 clove garlic
3 tomatoes
50 g (2 oz) mushrooms
45 ml (3 tablespoons) chicken
stock
15 ml (1 tablespoon) tomato
purée
15 ml (1 tablespoon) sherry

Season the chicken joints and cook them in the oil until golden. Add the chopped onion and crushed garlic and cook them until the onion is soft and golden. Drain off any excess oil. Peel and chop the tomatoes and slice the mushrooms. Add them to the pan and stir in the stock, tomato purée and sherry. Cover and simmer for 45 minutes.

Chicken Paprika

4 chicken joints
40 g (1½ oz) seasoned flour
200 g (8 oz) onions
50 g (2 oz) butter
15 ml (1 tablespoon) paprika
125 ml (¼ pint) tomato juice
5 ml (1 teaspoon) sugar
5 ml (1 teaspoon) salt
1 bayleaf
125 ml (¼ pint) yoghurt or
commercial soured cream

Skin the chicken joints and coat them with seasoned flour. Fry the chopped onions in butter very gently till soft but not brown. Move them to one side of the pan. Add the chicken and fry it for 5 minutes, until golden. Combine the paprika, tomato juice, sugar and salt and pour them over the chicken. Add the bayleaf. Cover the pan and simmer for 45 minutes. Transfer the chicken to a warm dish, stir yoghurt or sour cream into the sauce and reheat it, without boiling, for 3 minutes. Pour this over the chicken. Serve with potatoes, rice or dumplings.

Basic Chicken Curry

4 chicken joints
30 ml (2 tablespoons) oil
1 green pepper
30 ml (2 tablespoons) curry
  powder
15 g (½ oz) plain flour
500 ml (1 pint) chicken stock
1 lemon
salt and pepper
15 ml (1 tablespoon) mango
  chutney

Brown the chicken joints on all sides in the oil. Drain and keep them warm. Chop the onion and green pepper and cook them in the oil until soft. Stir in the curry powder and flour and cook gently for 3 minutes. Blend in the chicken stock and bring it to the boil. Add the grated rind and juice of the lemon, salt, pepper and chutney. Add the chicken and bring the liquid to the boil again. Cover and simmer for 45 minutes.

Serve the curry with boiled rice, poppadums, mango chutney and side dishes. Try thinly sliced cucumber in yoghurt; mixed chopped tomatoes and onions seasoned with lemon juice; thickly sliced bananas in yoghurt, seasoned with lemon juice and sprinkled with de-siccated coconut; mixed salted nuts and raisins.

Chicken Biryani

4 chicken joints
125 ml (¼ pint) natural yoghurt
30 ml (2 tablespoons) curry
  powder
1 large onion
30 ml (2 tablespoons) oil
500 ml (1 pint) chicken stock
2 large potatoes
50 g (2 oz) long-grain rice
25 g (1 oz) sultanas
salt
1 hard-boiled egg
25 g (1 oz) toasted flaked
  almonds

Put the chicken pieces in a shallow dish. Mix the yoghurt and curry powder and pour it over the chicken. Cover and leave to stand in a cool place for 2 hours. Chop the onion and cook it in the oil until soft and golden. Lift out the onion and put it into a casserole. Put the chicken and sauce into the oil and fry for 5 minutes, turning the chicken often to prevent it sticking. Place the chicken and sauce in the casserole. Put the stock into the frying pan and bring it to the boil, stirring well to loosen any brown bits in the pan. Peel and dice the potatoes. Add the potatoes and rice to the stock, stir well and simmer for 5 minutes. Pour this over the chicken and add the sultanas and salt to taste. Cover and bake at 180°C (350°F)/Gas 4 for 1 hour. Garnish with thin slices of hard-boiled egg and a sprinkling of almonds. Serve with boiled rice, poppadums and mango chutney.

79

Tandori Chicken

4 chicken quarters
125 ml ($\frac{1}{4}$ pint) natural yoghurt
1 medium onion
2 cloves garlic
5 ml (1 teaspoon) ground ginger
30 ml (2 tablespoons) curry
  powder
5 ml (1 teaspoon) salt
5 ml (1 teaspoon) paprika
10 ml (2 teaspoons) vinegar
10 ml (2 teaspoons)
  Worcestershire sauce
juice of 1 lemon

Skin the chicken and prick the flesh well with a fork or skewer. Put it into a deep dish. Mix together the yoghurt, finely chopped onion, crushed garlic, ginger, curry powder, salt, paprika, vinegar, Worcestershire sauce and lemon juice. Pour this over the chicken to cover the pieces completely. Cover with foil and leave overnight. Put a wire rack into a roasting tin and place the chicken pieces on top. Brush any remaining yoghurt mixture on the joints. Bake at 180°C (350°F)/Gas 4 for $1\frac{1}{4}$ hours. Serve garnished with lemon slices and onion rings, and with some boiled rice and mango chutney.

Chicken with Cashew Nuts

4 chicken joints
250 ml ($\frac{1}{2}$ pint) stock or water
30 ml (2 tablespoons) oil
5 ml (1 teaspoon) chilli powder
2 cloves garlic
5 ml (1 teaspoon) ground ginger
15 ml (1 tablespoon) curry
  powder
2 large onions
250 ml ($\frac{1}{2}$ pint) natural yoghurt
100 g (4 oz) cashew nuts
salt

Simmer the chicken in stock or water until it is tender. Strain and reserve the stock. Heat the oil in a thick-bottomed pan and stir in the chilli powder, crushed garlic, ginger and curry powder. Add the finely chopped onions and fry them until soft and golden. Measure 125 ml ($\frac{1}{4}$ pint) stock and mix it well with the yoghurt. Add this to the onions and bring it to the boil. Add the chicken and simmer for 10 minutes. Stir well, add the cashew nuts and salt to taste and reheat. Serve with rice and chutney.

Indian Chicken

6 chicken joints
450 g (1 lb) onions
50 g (2 oz) butter
15 ml (3 teaspoons) curry
  powder
250 ml ($\frac{1}{2}$ pint) natural
  yoghurt

Wipe the chicken joints. Slice the onions thinly and fry them in the butter until soft and golden. Add the chicken joints and cook them until golden on all sides. Stir in the curry powder and fry this for 1 minute. Add the yoghurt, cover, and cook very gently until the chicken is tender. A very little water may be added, but the sauce should be thick. Serve with rice and chutney.

80

Cider Chicken Curry

4 chicken joints
30 ml (2 tablespoons) oil
25 g (1 oz) butter
1 medium onion
1 apple
15 g ($\frac{1}{2}$ oz) curry powder
5 ml (1 teaspoon) curry paste
15 g ($\frac{1}{2}$ oz) cornflour
125 ml ($\frac{1}{4}$ pint) stock
125 ml ($\frac{1}{4}$ pint) dry cider
salt and pepper
25 g (1 oz) sultanas
30 ml (2 tablespoons) single
  cream
squeeze of lemon juice

Fry the chicken joints in hot oil and butter until golden. Lift them out and keep them warm. Add the chopped onion to the fat and cook it until soft and golden. Peel and core the apple and chop the flesh. Add it to the onion and cook for 3 minutes. Work in the curry powder, paste and cornflour, and then add the stock and cider. Season with salt and pepper and bring to the boil. Add the sultanas and the chicken joints, cover and simmer for 30 minutes. Stir in the cream and lemon juice and serve with rice and side dishes.

Chicken and Fruit Curry

4 chicken joints
30 ml (2 tablespoons) oil
1 medium onion
2 cloves garlic
15 ml (3 teaspoons) curry
  powder
500 ml (1 pint) chicken stock
30 ml (2 tablespoons) mango
  chutney
225 g (8 oz) canned apricots
225 g (8 oz) canned pineapple
  cubes
1 banana
10 ml (2 teaspoons) arrowroot

Skin the chicken joints. Heat the oil and cook the sliced onion and crushed garlic until soft and golden. Stir in the curry powder and cook for 3 minutes. Add the chicken joints and brown them all over. Pour in the stock and add the chutney. Bring this to the boil and simmer for 30 minutes. Drain the apricots and pineapple and stir them into the pan. Add the thickly sliced banana. Heat this through and thicken the sauce with the arrowroot mixed with a little water. Serve with boiled rice coloured with a little saffron or turmeric. This is a particularly attractive dish for a small party.

Chicken Vindaloo

4 chicken joints
2 large onions
2 cloves garlic
50 g (2 oz) butter
5 ml (1 teaspoon) chilli powder
5 ml (1 teaspoon) ground ginger
30 ml (2 tablespoons) curry
    powder
30 ml (2 tablespoons) vinegar
250 ml (½ pint) water
5 ml (1 teaspoon) salt
50 g (2 oz) desiccated coconut

Skin the chicken joints. Chop the onions and crush the garlic. Cook them in butter until the onions are golden. Stir in the chilli powder, ginger and curry powder and cook gently for 2 minutes. Add the vinegar and water with the chicken pieces. Bring this to the boil, cover and simmer for 30 minutes. Take off the lid and boil the gravy rapidly until it thickens. Stir in the salt and coconut and simmer for 15 minutes. Serve with rice, chutney and poppadums.

Chicken and Lentil Curry

4 chicken joints
225 g (8 oz) lentils
500 ml (1 pint) water
2 medium onions
2 large potatoes
2 tomatoes
1 aubergine
30 ml (2 tablespoons) curry
    powder
juice of 1 lemon
5 ml (1 teaspoon) salt
15 ml (1 tablespoon) chopped
    mint

Skin the chicken joints and put them into a pan of boiling water together with the lentils. Chop and add the onions, potatoes, tomatoes and aubergine. Cover and simmer for 45 minutes until the chicken is tender. Drain it and remove the meat from the bones. Put the remaining ingredients through a sieve and discard the residue. Return the chicken and sauce to the pan. Cook for 15 minutes. Serve with rice, poppadums and chutney.

South African Chicken

4 chicken joints
pinch of salt
1 large onion
25 g (1 oz) butter
15 g (½ oz) curry powder
375 ml (¾ pint) chicken stock
15 ml (1 tablespoon) vinegar
*15 ml (1 tablespoon) apricot
    jam*
25 g (1 oz) sugar
25 g (1 oz) sultanas

Cover the chicken with water. Add a pinch of salt and simmer until tender. Drain off the liquid and measure out and retain 374 ml (¾ pint) to use in the recipe. Slice the onion finely and fry it in the butter until soft and golden. Add the curry powder and flour and stir for 1 minute. Gradually add the chicken stock, stirring until smooth. Add the vinegar, jam, sugar and sultanas and pour the sauce over the chicken. Cover and simmer for 30 minutes. This should be rather dry, but a little extra chicken stock may be added, if wished. Serve with boiled rice and side dishes of desiccated coconut, sliced bananas and tomato wedges.

Honey Chicken Curry

1.35-kg (3-lb) chicken
½ lemon
225 g (8 oz) clear honey
175 g (6 oz) tomato chutney
*15 ml (1 tablespoon) curry
    powder*
100 g (4 oz) long-grain rice
*30 ml (2 tablespoons)
    mayonnaise*
125 ml (¼ pint) double cream
10 ml (2 teaspoons) lemon juice

Roast the chicken with the lemon inside it at 180°C (350°F)/Gas 4 for 1¼ hours. Cool and joint the bird. Melt the honey and chutney with the curry powder in a pan. Bring it to the boil, simmer over low heat for 10 minutes and cool. Cook the rice for 12 minutes, rinse it in cold water and drain it. Line a dish with rice and arrange the chicken joints on top. Fold the mayonnaise, cream and lemon juice into the honey-curry sauce and spoon it over the chicken. Serve with banana slices, desiccated coconut and poppadums.

Pies and Puddings

Both fresh and leftover chicken can be extended by the use of pastry. Fresh chicken should be cut into small joints, while leftover cooked chicken can be diced or cut into neat pieces. When cooked in chicken stock, perhaps with milk or cream added, under a lid of pastry, the flavour becomes beautifully concentrated. Additional flavour may be given by fresh herbs, lemon rind or juice, vegetables such as leeks, peas, mushrooms and carrots and plenty of seasoning, while potatoes add flavour and extra bulk for hungry appetites.

Use shortcrust or puff pastry for these pies, well glazed with beaten egg or milk for a golden finish. The pastry may be homemade, frozen or prepared from a packet mix, but always allow time for it to cook completely, crisp and firm. If the filling is uncooked, it is a good idea to cook the dish for a short time at a high temperature to set the pastry, and then reduce the temperature to continue cooking. If the chicken is already cooked, a shorter time at a single temperature will be suitable. The filling for deep pies with a single crust can be quite liquid, consisting only of chicken stock or a thin sauce, but flans and small pies, to be eaten in the hand, need a firmer sauce to bind the ingredients. If it is felt that a pie may be rather dry, make up some extra sauce with chicken stock, or use a can of chicken or mushroom soup instead.

An old-fashioned suet crust is very good combined with chicken in a pudding or roly-poly, served with extra chicken gravy, or mushroom or parsley sauce.

Chicken and Sausage Pie

225 g (8 oz) pork sausagemeat
pinch of mixed herbs
25 g (1 oz) butter
350 g (12 oz) cooked chicken
25 g (1 oz) plain flour
250 ml (½ pint) chicken stock
salt and pepper
350 g (12 oz) shortcrust pastry
egg to glaze

Mix the sausagemeat with the herbs and shape it into 8 balls. Heat half the butter and fry the sausagemeat balls until golden. Put them into a pie dish and surround them with the chopped chicken. Add the remaining butter to the pan and work in the flour. Cook for 1 minute and then add the stock. Bring this to the boil, stirring well, and season to taste. Pour it into the pie dish and cool. Cover with pastry and glaze with beaten egg. Bake at 190°C (375°F)/Gas 5 for 30 minutes.

Chicken and Ham Pie

450 g (1 lb) cooked chicken
225 g (8 oz) cooked ham or
    bacon
3 hard-boiled eggs
salt and pepper
pinch of ground nutmeg
pinch of thyme
5 ml (1 teaspoon) chopped
    parsley
chicken stock
350 g (12 oz) puff pastry

Cut the chicken and ham or bacon into neat pieces. Put a layer of chicken into a pie dish, then a layer of sliced eggs and then ham. Follow this with another layer of chicken, eggs and ham. Season each layer with salt, pepper, nutmeg, thyme and a sprinkling of parsley. Cover with chicken stock, making sure it sinks down into the meat. Cover this with pastry and bake at 220°C (425°F)/Gas 7 for 40 minutes. Serve hot or cold.

Chicken and Parsley Pie

1.5-kg (3-lb) chicken
500 ml (1 pint) basin of parsley
500 ml (1 pint) milk
250 ml (½ pint) chicken or
    giblet stock
salt and pepper
225 g (8 oz) shortcrust pastry
125 ml (¼ pint) double cream

Joint the chicken and put the pieces into a pie dish. Fill the basin with washed fresh parsley. Chop the parsley and put it into a pan with the milk. Bring this to the boil and then mix it with the stock. Pour this over the chicken and season well. Cover with the pastry, making a small hole in the top of the pie. Bake at 220°C (425°F)/Gas 7 for 15 minutes, then at 180°C (350°F)/Gas 4 for 45 minutes, covering the pastry with a piece of foil if it gets too brown. When baked, pour the cream through the hole in the pastry and shake the pie gently to mix the cream with the other ingredients.

Chicken and Potato Pie

8 small chicken joints
3 large potatoes
2 large onions
salt and pepper
15 g (½ oz) plain flour
pinch of sage
pinch of thyme
5 ml (1 teaspoon) chopped
    parsley
chicken stock
350 g (12 oz) shortcrust pastry

Wipe the chicken joints. Peel the potatoes and onions and cut them into thick slices. Put a layer of chicken into a pie dish and cover it with some of the potatoes and onions, seasoning each layer with herbs and sprinkling it with salt, pepper and flour. Put in the remaining chicken, potatoes and onions, seasoning as before. Pour in the stock to just cover the layers. Cover with pastry. Bake at 200°C (400°F)/Gas 6 for 15 minutes, then reduce the heat to 180°C (350°F)/Gas 4 for 45 minutes.

Harold C. Palmer's Chicken Pie

450 g (1 lb) cooked chicken
450 g (1 lb) potatoes
250 ml (½ pint) chicken stock
250 ml (½ pint) evaporated milk
salt and pepper
chopped parsley
350 g (12 oz) shortcrust or puff pastry

Cut the chicken into dice. Peel the potatoes and cut them into small cubes. Arrange the chicken and potatoes in layers in a pie dish. The chicken stock should be rich and strongly flavoured – if you are using a stock cube, add some herbs to give it a richer flavour. Mix the stock and milk, and season it well with salt, pepper and plenty of parsley. Pour this over the chicken and potatoes and stir to mix it well. Cover with pastry and bake at 220°C (425°F)/Gas 7 for 45 minutes.

Harold C. Palmer was an American physiotherapist who, many years ago, as he alternately baked and pummelled my back, gave me some of his favourite recipes. This one has certainly given me many excellent meals and is one of the best pies I know.

Southern Chicken Pie

450 g (1 lb) cooked chicken
1 large onion
225 g (8 oz) pork sausagemeat
5 ml (1 teaspoon) thyme
5 ml (1 teaspoon) basil
salt and pepper
pinch of ground mixed spice
1 hard-boiled egg
450 g (1 lb) canned sweetcorn
50 g (2 oz) butter
75 ml (5 tablespoons) milk
10 ml (2 teaspoons) icing sugar

This pie has a 'crust' of sweetcorn which is a natural partner for chicken, and it makes a delicious change from traditional pies.

Cut the chicken into cubes. Chop the onion finely and cook it with the sausagemeat, herbs, salt, pepper and spice until soft and golden. Drain off the surplus fat which will have run from the sausagemeat. Put this mixture in the bottom of a pie dish and top it with slices of hard-boiled egg. Put on a layer of chicken. Drain the corn and simmer it with half the butter and milk and a little salt and pepper, until the corn is very soft. Mash the corn lightly and spread it over the chicken. Dot the remaining butter in flakes on the surface and sprinkle it with sugar. Bake at 190°C (375°F)/Gas 5 for 45 minutes. Serve with gravy and carrots or peas.

Chicken and Leek Pie

450 g (1 lb) cooked chicken
salt and pepper
4 medium leeks
375 ml (⅓ pint) chicken stock
100 g (4 oz) cooked ham or
  tongue
350 g (12 oz) puff pastry
egg to glaze
45 ml (3 tablespoons) double
  cream

Cut the chicken into cubes and put them at the bottom of a pie dish, seasoning them well. Clean the leeks and trim off the green stems. Slice these thinly and simmer them in the chicken stock for 15 minutes until tender. Drain off and reserve the stock. Put the leeks on top of the chicken and cover this with strips of ham or tongue. Pour in 250 ml (½ pint) reserved stock. Cover this with pastry, making a small hole in the lid, and glaze with beaten egg. Bake at 200°C (400°F)/Gas 6 for 40 minutes. Just before serving, warm the cream gently and pour it carefully through a hole in the centre of the pastry lid, gently tilting the dish to ensure that it penetrates.

Chicken and Egg Pie

1.5-kg (3½-lb) chicken
250 ml (½ pint) water
1 bayleaf
salt and pepper
25 g (1 oz) butter
1 medium onion
175 g (6 oz) button mushrooms
5 ml (1 teaspoon) mixed herbs
4 hard-boiled eggs
450 g (1 lb) shortcrust pastry

Put the chicken in a pan with the water, bayleaf, salt and pepper and bring it slowly to the boil. Cover and simmer gently until the meat is tender. Take the flesh from the chicken and chop it roughly. Skim the fat from the pan, remove the bayleaf and reserve the stock. Melt the butter and fry the chopped onion until soft and golden. Add the chopped mushrooms and cook for 2 minutes. Add the chicken and herbs and season to taste. Leave until cool. Roll out the pastry and line a 21 cm (7 in) deep cake tin with pastry. Spoon half the chicken mixture into the pastry case. Put the eggs on top and cover them with the remaining chicken. Put in 4 tablespoons chicken stock. Cover with the remaining pastry and seal the edges. Glaze with beaten egg and bake at 200°C (400°F)/Gas 6 for 30 minutes, then reduce the heat to 180°C (350°F)/Gas 4 for 30 minutes. Leave this to cool in the tin. Pour the remaining stock through a small hole in the lid and leave the contents in the tin until cold and set.

Giblet Pie

1 set chicken giblets
salt and pepper
plain flour
225 g (8 oz) stewing steak
1 large onion
2 hard-boiled eggs
350 g (12 oz) shortcrust pastry

Clean the giblets and cover them with cold water. Bring this to the boil and skim it well. Add the salt and pepper and simmer for 2 hours. Cut the giblets into small pieces and sprinkle them with a little flour. Cut the steak into small cubes, slice the onion thinly and cut the eggs in quarters. Fill a pie dish with the giblets, steak, onion and eggs. Cover this with the stock in which the giblets have been cooked. Cover with pastry and bake at 220°C (425°F)/Gas 7 for 45 minutes.

Chicken Jalousie

225 g (8 oz) cooked chicken
50 g (2 oz) button mushrooms
250 ml (½ pint) white sauce
salt and pepper
350 g (12 oz) puff pastry
egg to glaze

Dice the chicken and slice the mushrooms thinly. Mix this with the white sauce and season it well. Roll out the pastry to a rectangle 30 × 20 cm (12 × 8 in) and cut in half, across. Roll each piece of pastry to a rectangle 30 × 17.5 cm (12 × 7 in) and put one piece on a baking sheet. Fold the other piece in half, across the width, and, using a sharp knife, make cuts on the folded side to within 2.5 cm (1 in) of the cut edges. Open out the pastry, taking care not to stretch it. Pile the filling on the pastry base and damp the edges of the pastry with beaten egg. Place the pastry top carefully on the filling and seal the edges. Brush this with beaten egg and bake at 220°C (425°F)/Gas 7 for 40 minutes. Serve hot or cold.

Chicken and Mushroom Turnovers

350 g (12 oz) puff pastry
175 g (6 oz) mushrooms
15 g (½ oz) mushrooms
15 g (½ oz) butter
350 g (12 oz) cooked chicken
8 olives
125 ml (¼ pint) thick white
  sauce
1 egg

Toss the chopped mushrooms in butter. Add the mushrooms, chopped chicken and chopped olives to the white sauce and test for seasoning. Roll out the pastry thinly, to form four equal circles about the size of a saucer. Divide the mixture evenly among the circles and brush the edges with beaten egg. Bring up the edges to meet in the centre. Seal them all round and brush with the egg. Bake at 220°C (425°F)/Gas 7 for 10 minutes, then at 190°C (375°F)/Gas 5 for 30 minutes approximately. Serve hot or cold.

Autumn Chicken Puff

225 g (8 oz) puff pastry
450 g (1 lb) cooked chicken
salt and pepper
450 g (1 lb) cooking apples
15 g (½ oz) Demerara sugar
5 ml (1 teaspoon) ground
   cinnamon
5 ml (1 teaspoon) ground ginger
90 ml (6 tablespoons) water
½ lemon
60 ml (4 tablespoons) single
   cream
egg or milk for glazing

Roll out the pastry in a 25 cm (10 in) square and put it on a floured baking sheet. Cut the chicken into neat pieces and put them into a bowl with seasoning. Peel and slice the apples and put them into a pan with the sugar, cinnamon, ginger and water. Simmer until the apples are soft. Add the apple mixture to the chicken, with the grated rind and juice of the lemon and cream. Mix this well and put it in the centre of the pastry. Dampen the edges and fold in the corners, like an envelope. Seal the edges with a little beaten egg and glaze the surface with beaten egg or milk. Bake at 220°C (425°F)/Gas 7 for 15 minutes, and then at 180°C (350°F)/Gas 4 for 30 minutes. Eat hot or cold.

Chicken Curry Pies

350 g (12 oz) shortcrust pastry
1 medium onion
25 g (1 oz) butter
225 g (8 oz) canned apricots
10 ml (2 teaspoons) curry paste
10 ml (2 teaspoons) lemon juice
125 ml (¼ pint) commercial
   soured cream
2.5 ml (½ teaspoon) Tabasco
   sauce
salt and pepper
350 g (12 oz) cooked chicken
100 g (4 oz) cooked peas
egg to glaze

Chop the onion and cook it in the butter until soft and golden. Drain the apricots and weigh them out. Add the apricots to the onion and simmer for 15 minutes, to a thick pulp. Mix the curry paste with 1 tablespoon water and the lemon juice, and add this to the apricots. Stir in the soured cream, sauce, seasoning and chopped chicken and simmer for 10 minutes. Take off the heat, cool and stir in the peas. Use half the pastry to line individual tart tins and divide the chicken mixture among them. Cover each pie with a pastry lid and seal the edges. Glaze with beaten egg. Bake at 200°C (400°F)/Gas 6 for 25 minutes until golden. These make delicious little pies for parties, and leftover turkey can be used instead of chicken.

Little Chicken Pies

450 g (1 lb) shortcrust pastry
2 rashers lean bacon
275 g (10 oz) cooked chicken
250 ml (½ pint) white sauce
salt and pepper
pinch of nutmeg
juice of ½ lemon
2 medium carrots
50 g (2 oz) frozen peas

Make the white sauce before beginning on the pies, using strong chicken stock (add a chicken stock cube to give a stronger flavour if necessary). Roll out the pastry to make twelve circles and line large patty tins or foil cases with half the circles. Chop the bacon and heat it in a thick-bottomed pan until the fat runs and the bacon is golden. Add this to the chopped chicken and the sauce. Season this well with salt, pepper and nutmeg, and add the lemon juice. Cook the carrots and dice them. Add the carrots and peas to the chicken mixture and divide this among the six pastry cases. Top them with the remaining pastry circles and seal the edges firmly. Brush the tops with a little milk or beaten egg. Bake at 220°C (425°F)/Gas 7 for 20 minutes and then at 180°C (350°F)/Gas 4 for 20 minutes. Serve hot or cold.

Individual Chicken and Mushroom Pies

450 g (1 lb) cooked chicken
10 g (4 oz) mushrooms
2 hard-boiled eggs
1 medium onion
4 rashers streaky bacon
15 ml (1 tablespoon) vinegar
15 ml (1 teaspoon) chopped
   parsley
2.5 ml (½ teaspoon) salt
2.5 ml (½ teaspoon)
   Worcestershire sauce
chicken stock
250 g (12 oz) puff pastry
egg to glaze

Cut the chicken into cubes. Slice the mushrooms and chop the eggs, onion and bacon. Mix these together with the chicken, parsley, salt and sauce and divide among 4 individual pie dishes. Pour in the chicken stock to come halfway up the other ingredients. Cover this with pastry and glaze with beaten egg. Bake at 220°C (425°F)/Gas 7 for 25 minutes.

Chicken Vol-Au-Vent

350 g (12 oz) puff pastry
egg to glaze
225 g (8 oz) cooked chicken
40 g (1½ oz) butter
4 rashers lean bacon
100 g (4 oz) button mushrooms
25 g (1 oz) plain flour
125 ml (¼ pint) chicken stock
125 ml (¼ pint) milk
salt and pepper

Form the pastry into an oval and roll it out carefully to a length of about 20 cm (8 in). Put it on a baking sheet. Using a sharp pointed knife, mark line, 1.25 cm (½ in) from the edge, cutting halfway through the pastry. Glaze the pastry with beaten egg. Bake at 220°C (425°F)/Gas 7 for 20 minutes until golden brown. Remove from the oven and, with the tip of a knife, remove the lid.

Chop the chicken in small pieces. Melt the butter and cook the chopped bacon and quartered mushrooms for 5 minutes. Work in the flour and stir in the stock and milk. Bring this to the boil and simmer for 5 minutes. Season to taste and stir in the chopped chicken. Reheat and fill the centre of the pastry case. Put back the pastry lid and serve at once with vegetables. The same mixture may be used to fill individual vol-au-vent cases.

Chicken Liver Pies

4 chicken livers
25 g (1 oz) butter
200 g (7 oz) puff pastry
salt and pepper
125 ml (¼ pint) rich gravy
egg or milk for glazing

Cut the livers into small pieces and toss them in butter over a low heat for 5 minutes. Roll out the pastry and use half to line small patty tins. Put in some pieces of liver and season well. Add a little thick gravy to each one. Cover with the remaining pastry and brush the tops with a little egg or milk. Bake at 190°C (375°F)/Gas 5 for 30 minutes. Serve hot or cold.

Chicken Flan

225 g (8 oz) shortcrust pastry
1 small onion
1 eating apple
15 g (½ oz) butter
15 g (½ oz) curry powder
2 eggs
125 ml (¼ pint) milk
salt
175 g (6 oz) cooked chicken

Line a 20 cm (8 in) diameter flan tin with the pastry. Peel and chop the onion and apple and cook them in the butter very gently for 5 minutes. Add the curry powder, cook for 1 minute, and cool. Mix the beaten eggs, milk, salt and curry mixture. Put the chopped chicken into the pastry case and pour on the egg mixture. Bake at 200°C (400°F)/Gas 6 for 30 minutes.

Chicken and Tarragon Pie

450 g (1 lb) cooked chicken
2 eggs
125 ml (¼ pint) milk
5 ml (1 teaspoon) tarragon
grated rind of ½ lemon
salt and pepper
350 g (12 oz) shortcrust pastry

Cut the chicken into cubes. Beat the eggs and milk and mix them with the tarragon, lemon rind, salt, pepper and chicken. Roll out ⅔ of the pastry to line a 17.5-cm (7-in) diameter sandwich tin, leaving a small overlap. Put in the chicken mixture and top with the remaining pastry. Roll over the overlapping pastry and seal the edges. Make 6 radial slits about 2.5 cm (1 in) long from the centre of the pie and turn back the points to make a star. Bake at 200°C (400°F)/Gas 6 for 10 minutes and then at 180°C (350°F)/Gas 4 for 30 minutes. This is particularly good served cold.

Chicken Pudding

1.8-kg (4-lb) chicken
1 medium onion
1 clove garlic
15 ml (1 tablespoon) chopped
    parsley
1 bayleaf
salt and pepper

Suet Crust:
225 g (8 oz) self-raising flour
100 g (4 oz) shredded suet
pinch of salt

Make up the suet pastry by stirring the flour and suet together with a pinch of salt and then making this into a soft paste with cold water. Line a basin with ⅔ of this pastry. Cut the meat from the chicken and mix white and dark pieces of flesh. Put them into the basin with the chopped onion and garlic, parsley, bayleaf, salt and pepper. Add enough water or stock to come to the top of the meat. Cover this with the remaining suet pastry and tie a piece of foil on the top of the basin. Put the basin into a saucepan and pour in boiling water to come halfway up the side. Boil for 3½ hours, adding a little boiling water to the pan during cooking so that it does not boil dry. Turn the pudding out and serve with brown gravy or parsley sauce. If liked, some chopped cooked ham or bacon, or some herb-flavoured balls of sausagemeat can be added to the chicken.

Chicken Roly-Poly

450 g (1 lb) self-raising flour
5 ml (1 teaspoon) salt
150 g (6 oz) shredded suet
225 g (8 oz) cooked chicken
225 g (8 oz) chicken livers
225 g (8 oz) mushrooms
15 ml (1 tablespoon) dried
   marjoram
salt and pepper

Sauce:
50 g (2 oz) butter
225 g (8 oz) mushrooms
10 ml (2 teaspoons) cornflour
250 ml (½ pint) chicken stock
salt and pepper
5 ml (1 teaspoon) tomato purée

Mix the flour, salt and suet with cold water to make a firm pastry. Roll this into a rectangle. Cover the pastry with chopped chicken, liver, some mushrooms, marjoram and seasoning. Roll it up and put it on a baking sheet. Bake at 190°C (375°F)/Gas 5 for 45 minutes.

To make the sauce, heat the butter and lightly fry the sliced mushrooms in it for about 4 minutes. Blend the cornflour with a little stock, add this to the pan and cook for 2 minutes, stirring well. Add the remaining stock. Season and bring to the boil. Add the tomato purée and cook for 2 minutes, stirring well. Serve separately in a sauce-boat.

Baked Chicken Pudding

450 g (1 lb) cooked chicken
225 g (8 oz) sausagemeat
1 medium onion
1 egg
250 ml (½ pint) white sauce
75 g (3 oz) fresh white
   breadcrumbs
2.5 ml (½ teaspoon) mixed herbs
5 ml (1 teaspoon) chopped
   parsley
10 ml (2 teaspoons)
   Worcestershire sauce
salt and pepper

Mince the chicken and mix it with the sausagemeat and finely chopped onion. Then mix this with the beaten egg, white sauce, breadcrumbs, herbs, sauce and seasoning. The mixture should be soft and creamy. Put it into a greased ovenware dish and bake at 180°C (350°F)/Gas 4 for 1 hour. Serve this hot with gravy, and any leftovers cold with salad. A little chopped ham or bacon may be added to the mixture, and a little chutney is also a pleasant addition.

8   Soups

Soup is a wonderful byproduct of the chicken carcase. Stock may be made from a freshly cooked bird or from a cooked carcase and giblets. When a bird has been specially cooked for a fine soup, some of the flesh may be used in the soup and the rest will make two or three meals, either served cold, or with a sauce, in pies, or other made-up dishes. Chicken stock is always worth making from the remains of a bird – even if a soup is not planned in the immediate future, the stock can be stored in the refrigerator for a week, or frozen for future use – a few spoonfuls can be used for many other dishes as well as soup. If the stock is not stored in a refrigerator or freezer, it must be boiled every day and used as soon as possible. The flavour will become more concentrated when it is re-boiled. If stock is not available for soups, chicken stock cubes may be used, but these are very salty and allowance must be made for this when seasoning.

Good chicken stock will set to a jelly in a cold place, but for fine soups it will need clearing. To do this, strain the stock and bring it to the boil. Add 1 egg white, whisking all the time, and remove from the heat. Leave it to stand until all the froth rises to the top, and remove this with a spoon. Repeat the process if the soup is not clear. If chicken stock cubes are used for consommés or other dishes which require clarity, the liquid should be cleared by pouring them through a sieve lined with a double thickness of kitchen paper.

Basic Chicken Stock

1 chicken carcase
chicken giblets
1 small onion
1 stick celery
1 carrot
1 bayleaf
3 peppercorns
sprig of parsley
1.2 ml (¼ teaspoon) salt
1 litre (2 pints) water

Put all the ingredients in a large pan. Bring them to the boil and simmer for $1\frac{1}{4}$ hours. Take out the bones, giblets and loose meat and continue simmering for 20 minutes. Strain and keep in a cool place.

Chicken Consommé

1.5-kg (3½-lb) chicken
25 g (1 oz) butter
675 g (1½ lb) shin beef
1 onion
¼ celery head
2 carrots
1 leek
1 medium turnip
6 peppercorns
salt
1 bayleaf
2 sprigs parsley
2 cloves
5 litres (8 pints) water
60 ml (4 tablespoons) sherry

Brown the chicken all over in the butter. Add the veal knuckle and the beef, cut in pieces. Add the water and bring it slowly to the boil, then skim it well. Add the whole vegetables, herbs and seasonings and simmer gently for 2 hours. Take out the chicken (which can be used for other dishes). Remove the pan from the heat and skim off any fat from the surface. Continue simmering for 2 hours. Skim off the fat again and then strain the stock through a fine sieve. If it is not clear, clarify it with an egg white (see instructions at the beginning of this chapter). Stir in the sherry and serve hot or cold. If a firmer soup is required when cold, a little gelatine (about 1 tablespoon) may be used.

Cream of Chicken Soup

1 chicken carcase
750 ml (1¼ pints) water
salt and pepper
1 bayleaf
sprig of thyme
sprig of parsley
225 g (8 oz) carrots
100 g (4 oz) frozen peas
125 ml (¼ pint) milk
125 ml (¼ pint) single cream
chopped parsley

Remove any small pieces of meat from the chicken carcase. Put the carcase into a large pan with the water, seasoning and herbs. Simmer for 2 hours. Strain off the stock and put it into a clean pan with the vegetables and meat. Continue cooking until the vegetables are tender. Add the milk and cream and adjust the seasoning. Bring it to the boil and serve hot, sprinkled with chopped parsley.

Chicken Noodle Soup

1 litre (2 pints) chicken stock
salt and pepper
50 g (2 oz) cooked chicken
50 g (2 oz) noodles
30 ml (2 teaspoons) chopped
  parsley

See that the chicken stock is strongly flavoured — if necessary add a stock cube. Bring the stock to the boil and season it. Add the chicken, cut in dice. Simmer gently for 10 minutes. Meanwhile, cook the noodles in salted water according to the directions on the packet. Drain well and add this to the soup. Serve it very hot, garnished with parsley. Other kinds of pasta, such as spaghetti or vermicelli (broken in small pieces), or pasta shapes, may be used instead of noodles.

Old-Fashioned Chicken Soup

1 litre (2 pints) chicken stock
2 bayleaves
6 peppercorns
blade of mace
6 cloves
salt
1 small onion
30 ml (2 tablespoons) pearl
  barley
50 g (2 oz) cooked chicken
75 ml (3 fl oz) dry sherry
30 ml (2 tablespoons) chopped
  parsley

Put the chicken stock into a pan with the bayleaves, peppercorns, mace, cloves, salt and finely chopped onion. Bring it to the boil and then simmer gently for 30 minutes. Strain and return it to the saucepan. Add the barley and simmer for 1 hour. Just before serving, stir in the chopped chicken and heat it through. Remove the pan from the heat, and stir in the sherry and parsley before serving.

96

Chicken Curry Soup

3 chicken joints
1 medium onion
1 carrot
1 stick celery
1 bayleaf
sprig of parsley
sprig of thyme
piece of lemon peel
salt and pepper
30 ml (2 tablespoons) oil
30 ml (2 tablespoons) curry
  powder
5 ml (1 teaspoon) ground ginger
15 g (½ oz) plain flour
1 small apple

Put the chicken into a saucepan with the sliced onion, carrot, celery, herbs, lemon peel, salt and pepper. Cover with 1 litre (2 pints) water, bring it to the boil and simmer for 30 minutes, until the chicken is tender. Drain the chicken and cut off the flesh in small pieces, discarding the bones and skin. Heat the oil and cook the curry powder, ginger and flour for 3 minutes. Gradually stir in the cooking liquid from the chicken. Peel and core the apple and cut in thin slices. Add this to the stock, bring it to the boil and simmer for 10 minutes. Add the chicken pieces, reheat and serve hot.

Maryland Soup and Parsley Balls

1.35-kg (3-lb) chicken
1.5 litres (3 pints) water
1 large onion
1 medium carrot
1 stick celery
6 parsley sprigs
1 bayleaf
6 peppercorns
1 lean bacon rasher
15 g (½ oz) plain flour
salt and pepper

Parsley Balls:
2 eggs
5 ml (1 teaspoon) chopped
  parsley
50 g (2 oz) butter
salt and pepper
75 g (3 oz) self-raising flour

Put the chicken into the water with the sliced onion and carrot, diced celery, parsley, bayleaf, peppercorns and diced bacon. Bring this to the boil and then simmer for 3 hours. Cool and strain the liquid and take off any fat. Cut the chicken flesh into neat dice and return it to the strained stock. Mix the flour with a little of the liquid and stir it into the soup, with plenty of seasoning. Bring this to the boil and then simmer for 5 minutes.

Make the parsley balls by mixing the eggs, parsley, softened butter, seasoning and flour to make a soft dough. Drop a teaspoonful of the mixture into the simmering soup and cook for 5 minutes. Serve a few parsley balls in each bowl with the soup.

Chicken and Vegetable Broth

1.5-kg (3½-lb) chicken
1.5 litres (3 pints) water
1 carrot
1 turnip
1 leek
1 bayleaf
sprig of parsley
sprig of thyme
50 g (2 oz) lean bacon
salt and pepper
25 g (1 oz) pearl barley or rice
chopped parsley

Put the chicken into a pan with the water. Clean the vegetables and peel them. Put the peelings, outer leek leaves, bayleaf, parsley, thyme, bacon, salt and pepper in with the chicken. Bring to the boil and then simmer gently for 2 hours. Strain and discard the vegetable peelings and herbs. Take off the breast of chicken and dice it (keep the rest of the chicken for another dish). Return the chicken meat and liquid to the pan. Add the vegetables, cut in neat dice, and the barley or rice. Simmer until the vegetables are tender, adjust the seasoning and serve sprinkled with parsley.

Giblet Soup

1 set chicken giblets
1 small onion
1 stick celery
salt and pepper
25 g (1 oz) pearl barley or rice
chopped parsley

Clean the giblets and cut them in pieces. Put them into a pan with the sliced onion and celery, salt and pepper. Cover with 1 litre (2 pints) water and bring this slowly to the boil. Skim well and simmer for 1 hour. Add the barley or rice and continue simmering for 2 hours. Lift out the pieces of giblet and cut them very small. Return them to the soup, reheat, and serve sprinkled with chopped parsley.

Cock-A-Leekie

1.8-kg (4-lb) boiling chicken
chicken giblets
450 g (1 lb) leeks
100 g (4 oz) dried prunes
salt and pepper
50 g (2 oz) pearl barley or rice
   (optional)

Soak the prunes overnight. Put the chicken and giblets into a large pan and cover them with water. Bring this slowly to simmering point, season, and simmer for 1 hour. Clean the leeks and slice them thinly. Add them to the chicken, cover and simmer for 2 hours. Cut the prunes in half and remove the stones. Add the prunes to the soup and simmer for 30 minutes. Lift out the chicken giblets, and cut 225 g (8 oz) chicken meat into dice. Add this to the soup and serve hot. If pearl barley or rice is used, add it to the soup with the leeks. The remaining chicken and giblets can be used for another dish. Prunes may seem a rather odd addition to a savoury soup, but they are traditional in this very old Scottish recipe.

Chicken, Egg and Lemon Soup

1.8-kg (4-lb) boiling chicken
2 bayleaves
pinch of thyme
pinch of basil
pinch of salt
pinch of Cayenne pepper
5 ml (1 teaspoon) sugar
½ lemon
1 clove garlic
1 medium onion
1 medium carrot
2 celery sticks
50 g (2 oz) long-grain rice
3 egg yolks

Put the chicken into a large pan with water to cover. Add the bayleaves, thyme, basil, salt, pepper, sugar, grated lemon rind, chopped garlic, onion, carrot and celery. Cover and bring this to the boil, then simmer gently for about 3 hours until the chicken meat comes away easily from the bones. Strain off the liquid and put it into a clean pan. Chop the chicken meat finely and return it to the stock. Bring this to the boil and add the rice. Simmer for 20–25 minutes, until the rice is tender. Taste and add a little more salt and pepper if necessary. Whisk the egg yolks in a bowl with the juice from the lemon. Add a little chicken stock and stir. Put the soup on a very low heat and add the egg mixture, stirring all the time. Serve at once, as soon as it is hot.

Belgian One-Pot Soup

1.5-kg (3½-lb) chicken
1 lemon
2 carrots
3 leeks
4 sticks celery
2 medium onions
15 g (½ oz) butter
1 bayleaf
sprig of parsley
sprig of thyme
750 ml (1¼ pints) chicken stock
½ bottle dry white wine
salt and pepper
15 ml (1 tablespoon) chopped
    parsley
fried bread cubes

Rub the chicken all over with the cut lemon and put it into a saucepan. Slice the carrots, leeks, celery and onions finely. Melt the butter and cook the carrots for 5 minutes over a low heat. Add these to the chicken with the other vegetables, herbs, stock and seasoning. Bring this to the boil and then add the wine. Cover, bring it to the boil again, then simmer for 1½ hours until the chicken is tender (this may take a little longer if a boiling chicken is used). Discard the herbs. Lift out the chicken and cut the meat into neat pieces. Put the meat into a large serving bowl, boil the soup again and pour it into the bowl. Sprinkle the soup with parsley and plenty of fried bread cubes. This soup is really a complete meal and is very rich and satisfying. In Belgium, stale breadcrumbs are often used instead of bread cubes. A dish of boiled potatoes is sometimes handed around also, for each person to add to their helping of soup.

Queen Victoria Soup

25 g (1 oz) butter
1 small onion
100 g (4 oz) button mushrooms
2 sticks celery
750 ml (1½ pints) chicken stock
25 g (1 oz) tapioca
100 g (4 oz) cooked chicken
100 g (4 oz) cooked ham
pinch of sage
pinch of ground nutmeg
salt and pepper
2 hard-boiled eggs
125 ml (¼ pint) single cream
chopped parsley

Melt the butter and cook the finely chopped onion until soft and golden. Add the thinly sliced mushrooms and diced celery and cook for 10 minutes. Add the chicken stock, tapioca, chicken, ham, sage, nutmeg, salt and pepper and simmer for 20 minutes. Take the pan off the heat. Add the finely chopped eggs and cream, and reheat gently. Serve sprinkled with chopped parsley.

Chicken and Pork Chowder

1.8-kg (4-lb) chicken
100 g (4 oz) salt pork
225 g (8 oz) onions
8 cloves
2.5 ml (½ teaspoon) dried
    marjoram
1 bayleaf
salt and pepper
4 large potatoes
375 ml (¾ pint) milk

Cut the chicken into small joints. Cut the pork in small pieces and heat them gently until the fat runs. Put the chicken pieces into this fat and cook them until well browned. Put the chicken and pork into a pan. Slice the onions and cook them in the remaining fat until golden. Put the onions into the pan with the cloves, marjoram, bayleaf, salt and pepper. Rinse the frying pan with boiling water and pour the juices into the pan. Cover with water and simmer until the chicken flesh is tender and leaves the bones. Remove the bones. Peel and dice the potatoes and add them to the chicken. Simmer for 15 minutes. Stir in the milk and bring it just to the boil. Serve very hot.

Chicken and Watercress Soup

100 g (4 oz) watercress leaves
15 g (½ oz) butter
500 ml (1 pint) chicken stock
salt and pepper
1 egg yolk
45 ml (3 tablespoons) single
  cream
10 ml (2 teaspoons) chopped
  parsley

Wash the watercress and drain it well. Chop the leaves roughly and cook them in the butter over a low heat for 5 minutes. Stir in the stock, salt and pepper and simmer for 30 minutes. Mix the egg yolk and cream and stir in the chopped parsley. Add a little of the hot soup and stir well. Stir this into the rest of the soup and reheat, but do not boil. Garnish with cubes of fried or toasted bread.

Watercress and Potato Soup

450 g (1 lb) potatoes
1 large onion
50 g (2 oz) butter
1 bunch of watercress
750 ml (1½ pints) chicken stock
125 ml (¼ pint) milk
salt and pepper
pinch of grated nutmeg

Peel the potatoes and onion. Chop them roughly and cook them in the butter for 5 minutes. Remove some leaves from the watercress to use as a garnish. Chop the stalks and add them to the potatoes and onion. Continue cooking for 3 minutes, then add the stock. Bring this to the boil, cover and simmer for 20 minutes. Sieve or liquidize the soup. Add the milk, salt, pepper and nutmeg and reheat. Just before serving, stir in the reserved leaves.

Chicken and Tomato Soup

2 cooked chicken legs
1.25 litres (2½ pints) chicken
   stock
2 sticks celery
1 large carrot
5 large tomatoes
45 ml (3 tablespoons) tomato
   purée
juice of ½ lemon
salt and pepper
15 ml (1 tablespoon) chopped
   fresh herbs

This is a useful soup to make from boiled chicken, as the white meat can be used for another dish. Cut the chicken meat in neat pieces. Bring the stock to the boil and add the chopped celery and carrot. Cook for 8 minutes. Peel the tomatoes and remove the pips. Cut the flesh into strips and add this to the chicken stock with the chicken pieces. Add the tomato purée, lemon juice, salt and pepper, and simmer for 10 minutes. Stir in the herbs just before serving.

Chilled Chicken and Tomato Soup

900 g (2 lb) tomatoes
2 onions
1 clove garlic
2 potatoes
salt and pepper
375 ml (¾ pint) chicken stock
1 bayleaf
sprig of thyme
sprig of parsley
75 g (3 oz) cooked chicken
125 ml (¼ pint) double cream
chopped chives

Peel the tomatoes, onions, garlic and potatoes. Chop them finely. Put everything, except the chicken, cream and chives, into a saucepan. Bring this slowly to the boil and simmer the mixture for 30 minutes. Take out the herbs and either sieve or liquidize the soup. Put the soup into a basin, cover and chill it well in the refrigerator. To serve, pour the soup into glass dishes. Divide finely shredded chicken among the portions and stir it in. Spoon a swirl of cream on top of each and sprinkle it with chopped chives. Either set the glass dishes in chipped ice, or put an ice cube in each serving of soup.

Leek and Potato Soup

1 onion
4 leeks
3 medium potatoes
50 g (2 oz) butter
1 litre (2 pints) chicken stock
salt and pepper
30 ml (2 tablespoons) single
   cream
chopped chives

Chop the onion finely. Clean the leeks and cut them in thin slices. Peel and dice the potatoes. Melt the butter and cook the vegetables for 5 minutes until soft and golden. Add the stock, season, cover and simmer for 45 minutes. Stir in the cream just before serving, and sprinkle on the chives. The soup may be sieved or liquidized, and reheated before stirring in the cream and chives. If the soup is made with ¾ stock and ¼ milk, liquidized and chilled before serving, it is Crème Vichyssoise.

102

Victorian Giblet Soup

1 set chicken giblets
1 litre (2 pints) chicken stock
2 medium onions
bunch of fresh herbs
125 ml (¼ pint) dry white wine
25 g (1 oz) butter
25 g (1 oz) plain flour
salt and pepper
pinch of ground mace
juice of 1 lemon
2 hard-boiled eggs

Cut the giblets into small pieces and simmer them in the stock with the sliced onions and herbs until the giblets are tender. Strain off the liquid. Discard the onions, but mash the giblets. Use the meat from the neck, discarding the bones. Add the mashed giblets to the stock with the wine. Melt the butter and work in the flour. Stir this over a low heat until the mixture is a rich brown. Add a little of the soup liquid and stir until creamy, then add this to the remaining soup. Season well with salt, pepper and mace, and add the lemon juice. Simmer together for 5 minutes, then serve garnished with finely chopped eggs.

Chicken and Pea Soup

675 g (1½ lb) shelled peas
50 g (2 oz) butter
1 small onion
1 small lettuce
100 g (4 oz) spinach
sprig of parsley
salt and pepper
5 ml (1 teaspoon) sugar
750 ml (1½ pints) chicken stock
50 g (2 oz) cooked chicken
2 egg yolks
250 ml (¼ pint) single cream

Frozen peas may be used, and should be just thawed. Reserve 100 g (4 oz) peas and put the rest into a pan with the butter, finely chopped onion, shredded lettuce, spinach, parsley, salt, pepper, sugar and stock. Cover, bring to the boil and then simmer until the peas are soft. Sieve or liquidize this soup. Return it to the pan and simmer it for 10 minutes. Cook the remaining peas and add them to the soup with the chicken, cut in thin strips. Mix the egg yolks and cream in a bowl and add a little of the hot soup. Mix this well and stir it into the remaining soup. Reheat gently, but do not boil.

9   Mousses, Aspics and Salads

Cold chicken can, of course, be reheated in all kinds of sauces, or used in casseroles or pies, but often a second-day cold meal is required which is a little more interesting than a slice of chicken meat and a lettuce leaf. Chopped chicken makes delicious mousses with the addition of cream and aspic jelly or gelatine-set stock, and it can also be turned into more homely meat loaves and brawns. Whole chicken joints or large slices may be more elegantly finished by setting them in aspic or a creamy chaudfroid sauce. Packet aspic jelly may be used, but is improved with the addition of a little dry sherry. Homemade stock can be used to make the jelly, but must be carefully cleared for an appetizing effect (see Chapter Eight). If stock is made from cubes for these dishes, check the seasoning carefully, as the stock cubes may be heavily salted and will spoil the flavour of a delicate dish.

Chicken salads need to be in a creamy dressing, as cold poultry may be rather dry. The light and dark meat is best cubed or cut into neat bite-sized pieces and tossed in a flavoured creamy dressing before being arranged on salad vegetables.

Chicken Mousse

2 chicken joints
2 hard-boiled eggs
8 g ($\frac{1}{4}$ oz) butter or margarine
8 g ($\frac{1}{4}$ oz) plain flour
125 ml ($\frac{1}{4}$ pint) milk
salt and pepper
8 g ($\frac{1}{4}$ oz) gelatine
125 ml ($\frac{1}{4}$ pint) chicken stock
125 ml ($\frac{1}{4}$ pint) double cream
30 ml (2 tablespoons) chopped
  watercress

Poach the chicken joints in enough water to cover them, until tender. Lightly oil a ring mould and place the sliced eggs in the bottom. Melt the butter, stir in the flour and cook for 1 minute. Blend in the milk and cook until it becomes thick, stirring all the time. Season and cool. Liquidize the chicken with the stock and add it to the cool sauce. Melt the gelatine over a gentle heat and add it too. Stir in the whipped cream and chopped watercress. Season the mixture well then pour it into the mould and leave it in a cool place to set. Turn it out and fill the centre with any chosen salad.

Simple Chicken Mousse

225 g (8 oz) cooked chicken
vegetables and herbs for
   flavouring
250 ml (½ pint) chicken stock
8 g (¼ oz) gelatine
125 ml (¼ pint) double cream
salt and pepper
cucumber and tomato

Mince the chicken twice, using a fine grinder. Crush the carcase, add vegetables and herbs for flavouring (onion, carrot, parsley, thyme and bayleaf may all be used, barely cover it with water and simmer for about 1 hour. Strain the stock and reduce it to 250 ml (½ pint). Dissolve the gelatine in a little cold water over a pan of boiling water. Stir in the stock and add half of this liquid to the chicken meat. Half whisk the cream, until fluffy but not stiff. Fold in the chicken and seasonings. Transfer this to a serving dish and chill until set. Pour half the remaining jellied stock on the top and arrange on this a simple decoration of cucumber and tomato. Cover with the rest of the stock and leave to set.

Chicken and Almond Mousse

300 ml (12 fl oz) chicken stock
25 g (1 oz) gelatine
salt and pepper
1 thinly sliced onion
2 hard-boiled eggs
50 g (2 oz) almonds
225 g (8 oz) cooked chicken
200 ml (8 fl oz) double cream

Bring the stock to the boil. Dissolve the gelatine in a little cold water over a pan of boiling water. Cool the stock slightly and then put it into a liquidizer with the gelatine, seasoning, onion, chopped eggs, almonds and chopped chicken. Blend until smooth, gradually adding the cream to the mixture as it is blended. Pour this into a mould and chill until set. This mousse looks and tastes particularly delicious if a pattern of thinly sliced cucumber and blanched almonds is arranged on top when it has set, and then a little aspic jelly poured on top.

Chicken Salad Loaf

175 g (6 oz) cooked chicken
15 g (½ oz) gelatine
125 ml (¼ pint) chicken stock
salt and pepper
1 stick celery
6 stuffed olives
75 ml (3 fl oz) mayonnaise
50 g (2 oz) cooked peas

Cut the chicken into small pieces. Dissolve the gelatine in a little cold water over a pan of boiling water. Make up the gelatine to 125 ml (¼ pint) with chicken stock. Put it into a blender with the chicken and blend until smooth. Season well and add the finely chopped celery, sliced olives, mayonnaise and cooked peas. Mix this together well and put it into a mould which has been rinsed in cold water. Chill before turning out.

105

Jellied Chicken

1.35-kg (3-lb) chicken
450 g (1 lb) pig's trotters
1 large onion
salt and pepper
2 chicken stock cubes
5 ml (1 teaspoon)
   Worcestershire sauce
30 ml (2 tablespoons) tomato
   ketchup
25 g (1 oz) gelatine

Put the whole chicken, pig's feet, sliced onions, salt and pepper into a pan and cover with water. Simmer for 2 hours until the meat is cooked and the liquid much reduced. Take out the chicken and pig's feet. Strain the cooking liquid and measure out 750 ml (1½ pints), returning it to the pan. Strip the meat from the chicken and pig's feet. Put a thick layer of white chicken meat at the bottom of a mould. Mix the remaining chicken and pig's feet and put this into the mould. Return all the bones to the stock in the pan and simmer for 10 minutes. Strain and add the stock cubes, sauce and ketchup. Simmer this liquid to dissolve the stock cubes. Dissolve the gelatine in a little cold water over a pan of boiling water. Stir it into the stock and pour this into the mould with the meat. Leave until cold and firm before turning out.

Chicken Picnic Loaf

1.35-kg (3-lb) chicken
1 medium onion
15 g (½ oz) fat
100 g (4 oz) bacon or ham
225 g (8 oz) pork sausagemeat
60 ml (4 tablespoons) stock or
   milk
4 hard-boiled eggs
salt and pepper
30 ml (2 tablespoons) cranberry
   sauce
5 ml (1 teaspoon) chopped
   parsley

Cut all the meat from the chicken bones with a sharp knife. Use the bones to make stock. Chop the onion finely and fry it gently in the hot fat. Put the chicken meat, bacon or ham through a mincer, and add this to the sausagemeat and fried onion. Add seasoning, chopped parsley and cranberry sauce. Mix it all together with stock or milk. Grease a mould or 900-g (2-lb) loaf tin with butter and put one-third of the chicken mixture into the base. Place shelled hard-boiled eggs in a line along the top and cover with the rest of the chicken mixture. Cover with foil or greased paper and cook at 180°C (350°F)/Gas 4 for 1¼ hours. If a slightly browner top is required, remove the foil 15 minutes before the end of the cooking time. Serve cold with salad.

Chicken Aspic with Olives

1.5-kg (3½-lb) chicken
5 ml (1 teaspoon) tarragon
salt and pepper
50 g (2 oz) butter
500 ml (1 pint) aspic
100 ml (4 fl oz) sherry
slice of canned red pepper
black olives
green olives

Joint the chicken into 6 pieces and rub each portion with tarragon and seasoning. Brush them over with the softened butter and roast them at 200°C (400°F)/Gas 5 for 50 minutes, basting frequently. When tender and golden brown take them out and drain and cool them. Make up the aspic, according to the directions on the packet, with 400 ml (16 fl oz) chicken stock and the sherry, and cool it. Set half of the aspic in a square baking tin. When on the point of setting, brush the chicken joints with the rest of the aspic and leave them to set. Cut the pepper and olives, dip them in the aspic and decorate each joint. Brush them twice again with the aspic so that each joint is well covered, and leave them to set finally in the refrigerator. Turn out the aspic in the pan and cut in dice. Arrange the chicken pieces on a dish and garnish with whole olives and the aspic dice.

Chaudfroid of Chicken

8 chicken breasts
40 g (1¼ oz) butter
40 g (1¼ oz) plain flour
375 ml (¾ pint) milk
salt and pepper
100 ml (4 fl oz) aspic jelly
15 g (½ oz) gelatine
30 ml (2 tablespoons) double
    cream

Garnish:
750 ml (1½ pints) aspic jelly
8 asparagus spears
parsley
1 canned red pepper

Poach the chicken breasts and cool them in the liquid. Melt the butter and stir in the flour. Cook for 1 minute. Gradually stir in the milk and season well. Keep stirring over a low heat until the sauce is thick and creamy. Make up the aspic jelly from a packet and measure out 100 ml (4 fl oz), reserving the remainder for garnishing. Cool the white sauce. Add the aspic jelly with the gelatine dissolved in it, and the cream. Drain the breast well, set them on a wire rack and coat them with the sauce, twice if necessary. When set, decorate each breast with the asparagus, parsley and diamonds of pepper. Finally coat them well with aspic jelly and leave to be set. Cover a large dish with a thin layer of aspic and, when set, arrange the breasts on it carefully.

107

Chicken Brawn

1.5-kg (3¼-lb) chicken
½ salted pig's head
12 peppercorns
5 ml (1 teaspoon) salt
sprig of parsley
strip of lemon peel
1 medium onion
2 bayleaves
pinch of ground nutmeg
pepper

Put the chicken and giblets into a pan with the peppercorns, salt, parsley and lemon peel. Do not peel the onion (this helps to colour the finished dish), but add it to the chicken. Just cover the chicken with water and simmer for 2 hours. At the same time, put the pig's head into another pan and cover it with water. Bring it to the boil and drain it. Cover it again with fresh water and add the bayleaves and nutmeg. Simmer for 2 hours. Slice the chicken meat in neat pieces, and chop the pork from the head. Put alternate layers of chicken and pork into bowls, seasoning each layer with pepper. Mix the two cooking liquids and boil them together until reduced by half. Strain and pour this over the meat and leave it in a cold place to set.

Gourmet Chicken Salad

4 chicken joints
60 ml (4 tablespoons)
   mayonnaise
30 ml (2 tablespoons) double
   cream
10 ml (2 teaspoons) lemon juice
paprika
4 tomatoes
½ cucumber
cress

Poach or roast the chicken joints, then cool them and remove the skin and bones, keeping the portions as whole as possible. Arrange them on a flat serving dish. Mix the mayonnaise, cream and lemon juice and spoon this over the joints to coat them. Sprinkle lightly with paprika. Skin the tomatoes and cut them into thin slices. Arrange alternating slices of tomato and cucumber round the dish and garnish with cress.

Sunflower Salad

450 g (1 lb) cooked chicken
60 ml (4 tablespoons)
   mayonnaise
15 ml (1 tablespoon) savoury
   bottled brown sauce
125 ml (¼ pint) double cream
2 oranges
1 eating apple
¼ cucumber
1 spring onion
salt and pepper
lettuce

Cut the chicken into neat cubes. Mix the mayonnaise, sauce and lightly whipped cream. Divide one orange into segments. Peel and core the apple and cut it into slices. Dice the cucumber and slice the spring onion. Mix the orange, apple, cucumber and onion into the mayonnaise and season to taste with salt and pepper. Fold in the chicken. Arrange lettuce leaves in a bowl and top with the chicken mixture. Cut the second orange into eight sections and use them to garnish the salad.

Chicken Curry Salad (1)

450 g (1 lb) cooked chicken
1 small onion
2 sticks celery
1 large green pepper
125 ml (¼ pint) mayonnaise
50 ml (2 fl oz) single cream
salt and pepper
5 ml (1 teaspoon) curry powder
30 ml (2 tablespoons) vinegar

Cut the chicken into neat cubes. Grate the onion and chop the celery and green pepper very finely. Mix the vegetables together with the chicken. Stir the mayonnaise and cream together, season well with salt and pepper, and stir in the curry powder and vinegar. Stir this dressing into the chicken and vegetables to coat them well. Chill the dish in the refrigerator before serving on a bed of lettuce.

Chicken Curry Salad (2)

450 g (1 lb) cooked chicken
50 g (2 oz) blanched almonds
50 g (2 oz) sultanas
250 ml (½ pint) commercial
    soured cream
5 ml (1 teaspoon) curry powder
15 ml (1 tablespoon) chopped
    chives
pinch of salt
lettuce
tomatoes

Cut the chicken into neat cubes. Chop the nuts roughly. Put the chicken and nuts into a bowl with the sultanas. Mix the soured cream, curry powder, chives and salt to taste. Shred the lettuce and arrange it in a border on a dish. Edge the dish with sliced tomatoes. Pile the chicken salad in the centre.

Curried Salad Amandine

450 g (1 lb) cooked chicken
175 g (6 oz) sliced celery
1 medium onion
50 g (2 oz) toasted blanched
    almonds
lettuce
desiccated coconut
raisins

Curry Mayonnaise:
125 ml (¼ pint) mayonnaise
5 ml (1 teaspoon) lemon juice
2.5 ml (½ teaspoon) curry
    powder
2.5 ml (½ teaspoon) salt

Toss the chopped chicken, celery, sliced onion and almonds together. Mix the mayonnaise, lemon juice, curry powder and salt. Add the curry mayonnaise and mix well. Serve on crisp lettuce, topped with coconut and raisins.

Chicken and Pasta Salad

350 g (12 oz) cooked chicken
175 g (6 oz) pasta shells
50 g (2 oz) button mushrooms
45 ml (3 tablespoons) olive oil
15 ml (1 tablespoon) wine
    vinegar
salt and pepper
75 g (3 oz) French beans
100 g (4 oz) peeled prawns
4 small tomatoes

Cut the cooked chicken into bite-sized pieces and place them in a large bowl. Cook the pasta shells in a pan of boiling salted water with a teaspoon of oil, for 12–15 minutes. Drain them in a sieve and run cold water through them. Leave them to cool. Wipe and trim the mushrooms and slice them very thinly into a small bowl. Stir in the olive oil and vinegar and season with salt and pepper. Mix this well and leave it to marinate. Top and tail the beans and cut them into 2.5 cm (1 in) lengths. Cook them quickly in boiling salted water for 7 minutes, until tender. Drain and cool them under cold water and add them to the mushrooms.

Stir the mushrooms and the beans and their marinade into the bowl of chicken, together with the pasta shells. Add half the prawns. Pile this into a serving dish. Skin the tomatoes and cut them in quarters. Garnish the dish with the tomato quarters and the remaining prawns.

110

Chicken and Plum Salad

1.5-kg (3½-lb) chicken
450 g (1 lb) ripe plums
1 clove garlic
120 ml (8 tablespoons) oil
30 ml (2 tablespoons) wine
    vinegar
salt and pepper
pinch of mustard powder
tarragon

For this salad, it is best to roast a chicken and leave it to get cold before carving, as it will then be very tender and juicy. Failing this, the salad is also very good when served with leftover cold chicken.

Cut the plums in half and put them into a bowl well rubbed with the cut garlic clove. Mix the oil and vinegar and season it with salt, pepper and mustard. Pour this over the plums and chill them. Just before serving, garnish this mixture with tarragon. A variation of this dish can be made using stoned, black, eating cherries and walnut halves in the same dressing.

Chicken and Rice Salad (1)

450 g (1 lb) cooked chicken
45 ml (3 tablespoons) olive oil
salt and pepper
pinch of ground nutmeg
squeeze of lemon juice
8 button mushrooms
1 green or red pepper
1 clove garlic
225 g (8 oz) cooked long-grain
    rice

Cut the chicken into large chunks and put them into a bowl with half the olive oil. Season well with salt, pepper, nutmeg and lemon juice. Slice the mushrooms thinly and put them into another bowl with the thinly sliced pepper and the remaining olive oil. Season this with salt, pepper, nutmeg and lemon juice. Add the crushed garlic. Leave the mixture in a cold place for 4 hours. Just before serving, mix the contents of both bowls with the rice and put this on to a serving dish.

Winter Chicken Salad

350 g (12 oz) cooked chicken
3 sticks celery
4 eating apples
75 g (3 oz) walnuts
30 ml (2 tablespoons) lemon
    juice
125 ml (¼ pint) mayonnaise
60 ml (4 tablespoons) double
    cream
chicory or endive

Chop the chicken and the celery. Do not peel the apples, but remove the cores. Dice the apples and toss them in the lemon juice. Mix the chicken, celery, apples and walnuts broken in pieces. Mix the mayonnaise and cream and pour it over the chicken mixture. Arrange the whole on a bed of chicory or endive.

111

Mediterranean Salad

350 g (12 oz) cooked chicken
225 g (8 oz) cooked rice
1 stick celery
100 g (4 oz) button mushrooms
50 g (2 oz) black olives
100 g (4 oz) grapes
5 ml (1 teaspoon) salt
1.2 ml ($\frac{1}{4}$ teaspoon) pepper
2.5 ml ($\frac{1}{2}$ teaspoon) rosemary
90 ml (6 tablespoons) oil
45 ml (3 tablespoons) vinegar
1 clove garlic
lettuce

Dice the chicken neatly and mix it with the rice, finely chopped celery and thinly sliced mushrooms. Add the olives and seeded grapes. Mix the salt, pepper, rosemary, oil, vinegar and crushed garlic and pour this over the chicken mixture. Line a bowl with shredded lettuce and put in the chicken salad.

Chicken and Rice Salad (2)

175 g (6 oz) long-grain rice
225 g (8 oz) frozen peas or
    mixed vegetables
50 g (2 oz) sultanas
225 g (8 oz) cooked chicken
90 ml (6 tablespoons)
    mayonnaise
60 ml (4 tablespoons) single
    cream
1.2 ml ($\frac{1}{4}$ teaspoon) curry
    powder
2.5 ml ($\frac{1}{2}$ teaspoon) salt
watercress

Cook the rice in boiling salted water for 6 minutes. Add the frozen vegetables and sultanas and continue cooking for 6 minutes. Drain and cool. Cut the chicken into neat cubes and mix them with the cool rice and vegetables. Mix the mayonnaise, cream, curry powder and salt and stir this into the chicken. Put the mixture into a serving bowl and garnish it with watercress. A few cubes of fresh or canned pineapple are delicious in this salad.

Kitchen Garden Salad

450 g (1 lb) cooked chicken
2 hard-boiled eggs
50 g (2 oz) stuffed olives
1 green pepper
2 tomatoes
½ small cauliflower
1 small lettuce
125 ml (¼ pint) olive oil
60 ml (4 tablespoons) lemon
juice
5 ml (1 teaspoon) chopped mint
salt and pepper

Cut the chicken into neat strips. Slice the eggs, olives, pepper and tomatoes. Cut the cauliflower in small pieces and shred the lettuce. Mix this together in a bowl. Mix together the oil, lemon juice, mint and seasoning and leave it to stand for 1 hour. Stir the dressing into the salad just before serving.

Chicken Cocktail

450 g (1 lb) cooked chicken
250 ml (½ pint) mayonnaise
30 ml (2 tablespoons) tomato
sauce
30 ml (2 tablespoons) lemon
juice
5 ml (1 teaspoon)
Worcestershire sauce
5 ml (1 teaspoon) curry powder
salt and pepper
1 lettuce
¼ cucumber
paprika

Cut the chicken into neat strips. Mix the mayonnaise, tomato sauce, lemon juice, Worcestershire sauce, curry powder, salt and pepper. Stir in the chicken pieces. Shred the lettuce and divide it among four glasses. Dice the cucumber and mix it with the lettuce. Pile the chicken mixture into the glasses. Sprinkle with paprika.

10   Pâtés and Terrines

Chicken livers and chicken meat both make excellent pâté, but there is an art in blending the ingredients into a deliciously flavoured mixture with a clearly defined texture. Too often 'chicken liver pâté' is dark and bitter, when it should be pale, creamy and savoury.

There is often confusion between the words 'pâté' and 'terrine'. Briefly, pâté is the actual meat mixture, and the terrine is a covered dish in which it is slowly cooked (in early days, this was a thick pastry crust which was discarded). The terms are often interchanged, but when the meat mixture is called a 'terrine', it usually indicates a coarse-textured pâté which is often a mixture of minced and cubed or sliced meat arranged in layers, and most suitable for serving in slices with salads or hot potatoes. A pâté may be smooth, or slightly chunky and juicy. Whatever you call the finished result, it should be made with good fresh ingredients, carefully seasoned, at least a day in advance so that the flavours blend and mature.

Some chicken liver pâtés consist of the lightly cooked livers mixed with butter or cream cheese and pressed into a serving dish without further cooking, and this is, in effect, merely a savoury paste. For a more robust pâté which is to be cooked, a proportion of fat is necessary, usually in the form of pork, bacon or sausagemeat, because, without fat, a pâté can be dry, crumbly and dull. Breadcrumbs may be added to give texture, and an egg used to bind the mixture.

Careful seasoning is vital to a good pâté. Salt and freshly ground pepper are obvious atlditions, but a pinch of ground mace or nutmeg helps to bring out the other flavours. Crushed garlic may be used, or fresh herbs, and a little brandy, dry sherry or reduced cider gives a special flavour.

The finished mixture should be cooked in a deep earthenware dish, a soufflé dish, or an ovenglass container. A special pâté dish in enamelled cast iron is useful, and looks attractive when serving. A loaf tin or round cake tin may be used, with a covering of foil, but when the pâté has cooled and firmed up, it may leave a stain on a metal container of this type. For cooking, the container should be placed in a roasting tin half-filled with hot water, and cooked in a low to moderate oven, so that the mixture is cooked through evenly, without hard over-cooked patches, and remains moist. To tell if a pâté is cooked, stick in a skewer. The juices should run clear, without any blood, and the fat should be transparent, without a pinkish tinge. The pâté will shrink in cooking.

Pâté should be cut neatly when cold, so it is important to finish it correctly after cooking. Put a flat board or dish on top of the cooked mixture and weight it evenly with scale weights or tins of food until cold and set. This will press out air bubbles and give a closer texture. The top of the pâté may be finished with aspic, melted butter or lard, but aspic should only be used if the dish is to be used up at one or two meals. If the pâté is completely sealed with fat, it will keep refrigerated for about a week, but should not be stored this way if it has a high bread content, or a lot of jellied juices surrounding the meat. Pâté may be frozen, but is best kept no longer than 2 months, like other cooked meat dishes.

Serve these pâtés with hot toast, biscuits, crusty bread or salad as a first course, or as the main part of a meal.

Chicken Liver Pâté (1)

225 g (8 oz) chicken livers
75 g (3 oz) fat bacon
1 small onion
2 cloves garlic
25 g (1 oz) butter
1 egg
salt and pepper

Cut the chicken livers, bacon and onion into small pieces. Cook the bacon, onion and crushed garlic in the butter until the onion is soft and golden. Stir in the chicken livers and cook for 5 minutes, stirring well. Put them through a sieve, or blend in a liquidizer. Mix this with the egg and season well. Put the mixture into an ovenware container and stand it in a roasting tin of water. Cook at 180°C (350°F)/Gas 4 for 1 hour. Cool under a weight.

Chicken Liver Pâté (2)

225 g (8 oz) chicken livers
50 g (2 oz) butter
30 ml (2 tablespoons) Madeira
    or port
salt and pepper
1 clove garlic
pinch of thyme

Fry the chicken livers in the butter until firm, but still pink inside. Mash and pound them until smooth. Warm the butter with the brandy and Madeira or port and mix this with the liver, seasoning, crushed garlic and thyme. Mix it all thoroughly and put it into small pots. Chill before serving. If a little clarified butter is poured on top to seal the pâté, it will keep in the refrigerator for 2 weeks.

Chicken Liver Pâté (3)

225 g (8 oz) chicken livers
4 rashers unsmoked streaky
  bacon
1 small onion
75 g (3 oz) butter
1 clove garlic
15 ml (1 tablespoon) brandy
pinch of thyme
pinch of ground mixed spice
1 bayleaf
a little melted butter

Cut the livers into small pieces. Chop the bacon and onion finely and cook them in 25 g (1 oz) butter until the onion is soft and golden. Add the crushed garlic clove and the chicken livers and cook gently until the livers are coloured, but still pink inside. Put this into a liquidizer and blend with thyme and spice until smooth. Soften the remaining butter and add it to the liquidizer until it is blended into the pâté. Press the mixture into a serving dish and put the bayleaf on top. Pour on enough melted butter to cover, and chill before serving.

Chicken Liver and Cider Pâté

250 ml (½ pint) cider
1 small onion
225 g (8 oz) chicken livers
salt and pepper
pinch of thyme
25 g (1 oz) fresh breadcrumbs
chopped parsley

Put the cider into a pan with the finely chopped onion and simmer until the onion is soft. Add the chicken livers and cook gently for 10 minutes. Strain and reserve the liquid. Mince the onion and liver or chop them together very finely. Season with salt, pepper and thyme. Boil the reserved liquid until 5 tablespoons remain. Add this to the liver mixture with the breadcrumbs. Press the mixture into a serving dish and sprinkle chopped parsley on top.

Chicken and Bacon Pâté

150 g (6 oz) cooked chicken
4 rashers bacon
1 small onion
75 g (3 oz) full fat soft cheese
2.5 ml (½ teaspoon) mixed herbs
salt and pepper
15 ml (1 tablespoon) sherry

Cut the chicken into pieces. Grill the bacon until cooked but not crisp and cut it into pieces. Chop the onion. Put all the ingredients into a liquidizer and blend until smooth. Press this into a serving dish.

116

Chicken and Ham Pâté

25 g (1 oz) butter
1 small onion
25 g (1 oz) plain flour
250 ml (½ pint) milk
salt and pepper
pinch of ground nutmeg
175 g (6 oz) cooked chicken
175 g (6 oz) cooked ham
sprig of parsley
2.5 ml (½ teaspoon) made
    mustard
2.5 ml (½ teaspoon)
    Worcestershire sauce

Melt the butter and cook the finely chopped onion until soft and golden. Work in the flour and cook for 1 minute. Slowly stir in the milk and cook until smooth and creamy. Season well with salt and pepper. Add the chopped chicken, ham, parsley, mustard and sauce and put everything into a liquidizer. Blend until smooth, put the mixture into a serving dish, and chill before serving.

Chicken Terrine (1)

250 ml (½ pint) dry cider
225 g (8 oz) streaky bacon
    rashers
350 g (12 oz) cooked chicken
225 g (8 oz) pork sausagemeat
1 small onion
1 clove garlic
25 g (1 oz) fresh breadcrumbs
1 egg
salt and pepper

Put the cider into a pan and bring it to the boil. Boil until reduced to 45 ml (3 tablespoons). Remove the rind from the bacon and flatten the rashers with a broad-bladed knife. Line a 900-g (2-lb) loaf tin with the bacon. Mince 100 g (4 oz) chicken and cut the rest into thin slices. Mix the minced chicken with the minced livers, sausagemeat, finely chopped onion, crushed garlic, breadcrumbs, egg, seasoning and cider. Put a layer of sliced chicken into the loaf tin, then a layer of minced ingredients. Continue in layers, ending with sliced chicken. Wrap the ends of the bacon rashers over the meat. Cover the top with foil and put the container in a roasting tin with some water. Bake at 170°C (325°F)/Gas 3 for 2½ hours. Drain off any excess fat. Cool the terrine under weights. Serve cut into slices.

117

Chicken Terrine (2)

1.5-kg (3½-lb) chicken
225 g (8 oz) cooked tongue
squeeze of lemon juice
75 g (3 oz) fresh breadcrumbs
1 small onion
salt and pepper
pinch of ground mace
5 ml (1 teaspoon) chopped sage
1 egg yolk
60 ml (4 tablespoons) stock
225 g (8 oz) cooked ham

Skin the chicken and take off the breasts. Cut the breast meat into thin slices and put it into a bowl. Squeeze lemon juice over it and season with salt and pepper. Mince the dark meat from the chicken with the tongue. Mix this with the breadcrumbs, very finely chopped onion, seasoning, mace and sage, and add the egg yolk and stock. Line a container with thin slices of ham, and if there is any left over, cut it into thin shreds and mix it with the minced meat. Continue in layers of chicken and minced tongue, ending with some of the minced mixture. Cover the top with foil and put the container in a roasting tin of water. Bake at 170°C (325°F)/Gas 3 for 1½ hours. Cool under weights. Serve cut into slices.

11   Turkey

Turkey used to be a traditional Christmas treat, or the obvious choice when catering for a large party, but it was never considered to be a family meal because of its sheer size. Today's production methods have resulted in a wide variety of birds to suit every need, so that even the small family can enjoy a mini-turkey, weighing about 3 kg (6 lb). Now that one family in five owns a freezer, it is also possible to store smaller birds ready for use whenever a party is expected, or for a celebration meal, and the turkey need no longer be eaten only in the middle of winter. For family meals, turkey is popular for its delicious flavour and the economy of the many dishes which can be produced from even a small bird. In addition, turkey has a higher protein content, and has fewer calories, than any other meat, and has also a low cholesterol count.

While most of us enjoy the traditional roast bird with its accompaniments of roast potatoes, cranberry sauce, bread sauce, sausages, bacon rolls and a variety of vegetables, the rich flavour of turkey may be complemented by herbs, spices and fruit, and it is worth experimenting with stuffings and dishes made from leftovers to find some exciting new flavour combinations. Recipes for stuffings and other accompaniments may be found in Chapter Three.

PREPARING A TURKEY FOR ROASTING

There is an art in cooking a fresh turkey or a completely thawed frozen one, and everyone has a theory about cooking a large bird. Some people get up in the middle of the night to cook a bird for long hours at a very low temperature. Others prefer a high temperature and short cooking time. The British Turkey Federation recommends cooking in a pre-heated moderate oven at 180°C (350°F)/Gas 4 with the turkey breast down on a special roasting rack in the tin, or else breast uppermost on a flat rack in the tin. To prevent drying out, loosely cover the bird with a tent of foil or greaseproof paper, but remove this about 30 minutes before the end of cooking time so that the breast browns. If additional fat is required for cooking, butter gives the best flavour.

Turkey should be allowed to stand for a few minutes before carving, so that the flesh sets firmly. If meat is to be served cold, the carcase should be cooled as quickly as possible. When turkey is to be reheated, care should be taken that the meat, as well as any sauce or gravy, is thoroughly heated through.

FROZEN OVEN-READY TURKEYS

These should be thawed completely before cooking. Follow the directions on the bag, but, as a general guide, this takes approximately 48 hours at room temperature or slightly less if the bird's weight is under 7 kg (16 lbs). If you wish to thaw the turkey more quickly, it can be immersed in cool running water. Remove the giblets and neck which can be used to make stock or gravy. Sprinkle the bird inside and out with salt and brush it with oil or fat.

CLEAN PLUCKED TURKEYS

After dressing and trussing, treat it in the same way as other thawed oven-ready birds. The oven-ready weight (used below for calculating cooking times) should be about $\frac{5}{6}$ of the clean plucked weight.

STUFFING

Stuffing in the neck cavity only, is recommended, or it may be cooked separately, outside the bird. Do not stuff the bird until it is ready for cooking. Do not stuff the body cavity. Tests have shown that this stuffing may not be adequately cooked by the time the meat is done.

COOKING TIME AND TEMPERATURE

Because of variations between ovens, the following times are approximate. Check towards the end of the cooking time. The turkey is cooked when the juices run clear when tested with a sharp skewer inserted in the thigh. Follow the directions on the bag for frozen turkeys. Partial cooking, with completion some hours later, is a practice that should be avoided.

Oven-ready Weight	Time at 180°C (350°F)/Gas 4
6.5 kg (15 lb)	$4\frac{1}{4}$ hrs
9 kg (20 lb)	5 hrs
11 kg (25 lb)	$5\frac{1}{2}$ hrs
13.5 kg (30 lb)	6 hrs

120

Size	Servings	*Portion Guide Thawing Time (Hrs) in Refrigerator*	*Oven*	*Roasting Time*
kg (lb)				
2.2–4 (5–8)	6–10	24–36	180°C (350°F)/ Gas 4	2 hrs 40 mins
4–5 (8–11)	10–15	36–42	180°C (350°F)/ Gas 4 for first hour, reducing to 170°C (325°F)/ Gas 3 for remaining time	2 hrs 40– 3 hrs 35 mins
5–6 (11–13)	14–18	42–48	180°C (350°F)/ Gas 4 for first hour reducing to 170°C (325°F)/ Gas 3 for remaining time	3 hrs 35– 4 hrs 05 mins
6–9 (13–20)	18–28	48–60	180°C (350°F)/ Gas 4 for first hour, reducing to 170°C (325°F)/ Gas 3 for remaining time	4 hrs 05– 5 hrs 30 mins

Turkey in a Salt Crust

2.2–3.6-kg (5–8-lb) turkey
100 g (4 oz) butter or margarine
15 ml (1 tablespoon) grated
   lemon rind
1 shallot
4 whole cloves
5 ml (1 teaspoon) thyme
5 ml (1 teaspoon) marjoram
1½ kg (3 lb) coarse salt

Wash the turkey well inside and out. Dry it with paper towels. Put 2 tablespoons butter, the lemon peel, shallot, cloves and half the thyme and marjoram inside the turkey. Close the opening with skewers. Brush the turkey all over with the rest of the butter. Sprinkle it with the rest of the thyme and marjoram. Put 450 g (1 lb) salt in the bottom of a large oval casserole. Sprinkle this with 250 ml (½ pint) water. Arrange the turkey on the salt. Cover it completely with the rest of the salt and sprinkle it with 500 ml (1 pint) water. Mould the wet salt to cover the turkey so that no skin shows. Bake uncovered at 230°C (450°F)/Gas 8 for 20 minutes per 450 g (1 lb) plus 20 minutes. The salt will form a hard crust. At serving time, take the casserole to the table. With a sharp knife, cut around the edge of the casserole. Lift off the crust. Lift the turkey onto a dish. If necessary, wipe off any salt with a damp paper towel. Carve the bird into serving slices.

Pressed Turkey for a Party

Turkey is a delicious meat for a party, with little waste, but it is often difficult to carve neatly into portions, or to get a fair proportion of white and dark meat. This method ensures that a turkey will serve a large number of people, and that the slices can be cut thinly.

Cook the turkey in foil so that the meat is cooked and tender, but not dry. Carve the meat in medium-thin slices and pack them into 1-kg (2-lb) loaf tins or rectangular casseroles, alternating dark and light meat. Fill the containers to the top and press the contents under heavy weights. The easiest way to do this is to cover a slightly smaller container with foil and put it on top of the meat with some canned food to act as a weight. This will give a neat even surface. Break up the turkey carcase and cook it in just enough water to cover it with plenty of salt, pepper and herbs. When the liquid is strongly flavoured and reduced by half, strain and pour it over the meat. Leave it to soak in and then press again. Leave it in the refrigerator until cold and firmly set. Turn it out on a serving dish and cut it in thin slices. Today's rolled turkey roasts may be used in the same way, using a mixture of those made from white and dark meat. As stock will not be available, it is best to use a can of chicken consommé which will set when cold. This is, of course, more expensive than using a traditional turkey. It is obviously possible to use some slices from a bird for family meals, and then prepare the pressed turkey from the leftovers which makes this a good method of dealing with a large Christmas turkey if a party has to be catered for at a later date.

Turkey Portions

Although everybody loves turkey, it is not always possible for a small family to buy a whole bird. The turkey industry has, accordingly, developed a number of products which make good meals all the year round, and can give everybody a taste of turkey when they feel like it without having to organize a party. Among these special packs are wings, drumsticks, thighs and breasts which will make a single hot meal for 2–4 people according to the pack, and may even yield a second-day cold meal. The packs can easily be divided, so that a single drumstick or breast can be used and will provide a lean nutritious meal for one large appetite or two small ones.

One of the most useful packs is the turkey roll, made entirely of lean meat and covered with a thin layer of fat for roasting. These simple cylinders of turkey come in family and catering sizes and nothing can be easier to carve. Everyone has a fair distribution of meat, and any leftovers are excellent for sandwiches, salads or second-day dishes.

Portioning a Turkey

A turkey may be portioned at home. A bird weighing 4.5 kg (9 lb) will give useful-sized portions.

1 Remove the giblets from the completely thawed bird. With one hand hold the turkey firmly on a wooden board, or on a clean cloth on a work surface to stop it slipping. Pull a leg away from the body of the bird, stretching the skin. Using a sharp cook's knife, pierce the skin with the tip and saw through the skin between the leg and the breast. Press the flat of the knife against the carcase and bend the leg outwards until the joint at the base breaks. Slice through the meat around the leg joint, cutting down towards the parson's nose, to detach the leg joint. Cut off the other leg in the same way.

2 To separate the drumstick from the thigh, cut through the meat at the joint, to the bone. Hold the drumstick in one hand and the thigh in the other and twist to break at the joint. Cut through the joint with the knife, leaving thigh and drumstick separate. Pull the skin over the joints evenly if it is to be left on for cooking. Separate the other leg joint in the same way.

123

3 To remove the wing, make a slantwise cut with the knife a short way up one side of the breast, at the neck end. With poultry shears or strong kitchen scissors, cut down through the wishbone and ribs to detach the wing with a portion of the breast attached. Detach the other wing portion in the same way.

4 Before removing the breast meat, it is easier to cut through the ribs first, using poultry shears or strong kitchen scissors. Do this immediately under the breast on both sides of the carcase, to separate the breast in one piece from the backbone. Cut or break the backbone piece in two for easier handling when making stock.

5 To remove the breast meat, place the breast, cut side down, on the board, with the breastbone uppermost. With a sharp knife, cut through the skin just alongside the breastbone. With a sawing action, and keeping the blade edge near to the bone, gradually ease the meat cleanly away from one side of the breastbone, so that it comes away in one piece. Remove the meat from the other breast in the same way.

6 There should now be 2 wings, 2 drumsticks, 2 thighs, 2 boned breast portions, 1 set of giblets and the carcase. The joints are now ready for cooking. If necessary, wrap them in foil and store them overnight in the refrigerator until you have time to finish cooking.

Stuffed Drumsticks

Choose large drumsticks and remove the bones and tendons without breaking the skin. Fill the cavity in each with the chosen stuffing. Keep the drumsticks their usual shape and close the opening at the end of each with a cocktail stick. Place them in a casserole, with stock, and bake at 180°C (350°F)/Gas 4 for 1 hour, until tender. Serve with bread sauce, cranberry sauce, gravy and vegetables. A large drumstick can be used to serve 2 people.

Little Turkey Pies

450 g (1 lb) turkey fillet
1 small onion
25 g (1 oz) cooking fat
165-g (5½-oz) can condensed
  mushroom soup
salt and pepper
675 g (1½ lb) shortcrust pastry
1 egg

Mince the turkey meat with the onion and fry it lightly in hot fat. Stir in the soup and simmer for 15 minutes. Season to taste. Leave the soup to cool. Roll out the pastry. Using 7.5-cm (3-in) and 8.25-cm (3½-in) cutters, cut the pastry into 24 rounds, 12, a little larger than the others, intended for pie tops.

Divide the cold turkey mixture between the smaller rounds. Dampen the edges of the pastry and top with the larger rounds. Seal the edges and flute or crimp them. Brush the pies with beaten egg and bake at 220°C (425°F)/Gas 7 for 25 minutes, or until golden brown. Serve hot.

Turkey Provençale

1 turkey roast (rolled and tied
   with string)
fat for roasting
oil for frying
300-g (11-oz) can sweet corn
1 red pepper
1 green pepper
12 black olives

Tomato Sauce:
50 g (2 oz) butter or margarine
1 carrot
1 onion
2 sticks celery
25 g (1 oz) plain flour
2 tablespoons tomato purée
250 ml (½ pint) stock
125 ml (¼ pint) white wine
salt and black pepper
1 bayleaf

Garnish:
sprigs of parsley
few black olives

Follow the instructions on the pack and cook the rolled turkey roast in some fat in a roasting tin at 180°C (350°F)/Gas 4 for 1 hour.

To make the tomato sauce; melt the butter or margarine and gently fry the chopped carrot, onion and celery until golden brown. Add enough flour to make a thick paste, then add the tomato purée and cook for 1 minute. Gradually blend in the stock and the white wine, season and cook over a gentle heat until thickened, stirring well. Add the bayleaf and simmer for 20 minutes. Strain this into a clean pan and keep it warm. Heat the oil and fry the chopped peppers until tender. Add the sweet corn and most of the halved olives and heat them through. Remove the turkey from the oven, slice it fairly thickly and arrange it on a serving dish on a bed of the peppers, sweet corn and olives. Pour a little of the tomato sauce down the centre of the turkey slices and decorate them with remaining black olive halves and sprigs of parsley. Serve the rest of the sauce separately.

Turkey Burgers

300 g (10 oz) fresh turkey meat
1 onion
10 ml (2 teaspoons)
   Worcestershire sauce
salt and pepper
pinch of mixed herbs
1 egg
oil for frying
4 soft baps or bread rolls
2 tomatoes

Mince the turkey finely. Peel the onion and chop it finely. Mix together the minced turkey, onion, Worcestershire sauce, seasoning and herbs until well combined, then add sufficient beaten egg to bind them. Pat this together into a ball and place it on floured surface. Divide it into four and shape each piece into a flat round cake. Heat the oil and fry the burgers until golden brown and cooked through (about 15 minutes depending on thickness). When cooked halve the baps, place a burger in each, and top each with a slice or two of tomato. Serve with a green salad.

125

Baked Turkey Galantine

450-g (1-lb) boned and rolled
    turkey joint
225 g (8 oz) herb sausages
1 medium onion
salt and pepper
100 g (4 oz) mushrooms
30 ml (2 tablespoons) chopped
    parsley
2 eggs
100 g (4 oz) fresh white
    breadcrumbs
2 hard-boiled eggs
250 ml (½ pint) stock

Put the turkey and sausage through the coarse cutter of a mincer with the onions and mushrooms. Add the seasonings, parsley and eggs and mix them together. Work in enough breadcrumbs to make a fairly stiff mixture. Take a length of aluminium foil, approximately 45 × 37.5 cm (18 × 15 in) and grease a 25 cm (10 in) wide panel. Put half the mixture in the centre of the panel, spread it out into an oblong, place the shelled eggs on top and then the remaining mixture. Sprinkle a few breadcrumbs on the top and form it into a firm roll. Bring the two ends of the foil parallel to roll them together and fold them over and over until they rest firmly on the roll. Fold up the other ends, place the roll on a baking tray and bake at 180°C (350°F)/Gas 4 for 1 hour. Open up the foil, replace the roll in the oven and turn the control to 220°C (425°F)/Gas 7 for 15 minutes, or until the outside is lightly browned. Overlap the foil over the galatine, place a board on top with about 1 kg (2 lb) in weights and leave it until cold. Transfer it to a serving plate. Boil the stock rapidly in an open pan until thick and syrupy. Brush this over the galantine and, when set, garnish it with some salad ingredients and decorate it.

Turkey Escalopes

4 turkey breasts
plain flour
1 egg
golden breadcrumbs
oil for frying
lemon slices for garnish

Using a heavy rolling pin, or steak bat, flatten the turkey breasts until very thin and double their oringinal size. Take care to keep them well floured on a board, as they break easily if sticky. Dust them with flour then dip them in beaten egg and then in the breadcrumbs until completely covered. Heat the oil and fry them for 5–10 minutes until cooked and golden brown. Serve them with slices of lemon and a fresh green salad. The turkey pieces may be cut in four before flattening to make *scallopine*, or little escalopes, which are ideal for a buffet party.

126

Summer Turkey Casserole

450 g (1 lb) turkey meat
oil for frying
1 large onion
3 carrots
25 g (1 oz) plain flour
15 ml (1 tablespoon) tomato
    purée
375 ml (¾ pint) chicken stock
250 ml (½ pint) milk
pinch of mixed herbs
salt and pepper
100 g (4 oz) shelled peas

Remove any fat from the turkey meat and cut it into cubes. Fry these in the heated oil until browned on all sides. Remove them from the pan, place them in casserole and keep them warm. In the remaining fat in the same pan, gently fry the chopped onion and sliced carrots until slightly browned. Remove and place these on top of the turkey pieces. Add enough flour to the fat in the frying pan to make a thick roux and cook this for 1–2 minutes. Add the tomato purée and mix it in well. Take the pan off the heat and gradually stir in the stock. Mix this to a smooth consistency. Mix in the milk and bring it to the boil, stirring well. Add the herbs and seasoning, pour the whole mixture over the meat and vegetables in the casserole and cook it at 170°C (325°F)/Gas 3 for 1 hour. Remove it from the oven, add the peas, replace it in the oven and cook for 25 minutes. Frozen peas may be used if necessary.

Turkey Kiev

2 turkey breasts
75 g (3 oz) butter
1 clove garlic
15 ml (1 tablespoon) parsley,
    tarragon and lemon thyme
15 ml (1 tablespoon) lemon juice
50 g (2 oz) plain flour
2 eggs
5 ml (1 teaspoon) oil
100–175 g (4–6 oz) dried white
    crumbs
oil for deep frying
lemon wedges for garnishing

Split the turkey breasts in half so that they remain the same size, but half the width. Flatten them out gently. Mix the butter with the finely crushed garlic, chopped herbs, lemon juice and seasoning, and shape this into a roll about 7.5 cm (3 in) long. Wrap it in foil and put it in the refrigerator to chill. Remove the skin from the turkey. Cut the butter into four pieces and place one in the centre of each piece of turkey. Fold the turkey round the butter like a parcel and secure them with cocktail sticks. Roll each in flour then beaten egg and then press the breadcrumbs round it until the turkey is well covered. Chill the pieces for 45 minutes. Brush them again with egg and then press on more breadcrumbs. Leave the turkey in a cool place for 1 hour before deep-frying in hot fat for 8–10 minutes, until golden brown and crisp. Serve with lemon wedges. For a change of flavour, use fennel instead of the other herbs. As the butter spurts out when the turkey is cut, make a neat incision with a sharp-pointed knife as each portion is served.

Turkey Thighs with Apricot Stuffing

4 turkey thighs
salt and pepper
1 small can apricot halves
100 g (4 oz) breadcrumbs
1 small onion
pinch of tarragon or sage
   1 egg
   25 g (1 oz) butter or
   margarine
10 ml (2 teaspoons) cornflour

Remove the bone from each thigh (or ask the butcher to do this) and leave each in a flat, oblong piece. Sprinkle them with salt and pepper. Make the stuffing, by draining the apricots and reserving the juice. Reserve 4 apricot halves for decoration and finely chop the rest. Mix these with the breadcrumbs, finely chopped onion and herbs and sufficient beaten egg to bind it together. Divide the stuffing among the four thighs and spread it over each in thinnish layer. Roll them up and tie them securely with string. Rub them over with softened butter or margarine, place them in a greased baking tin and cover it with foil. Roast them for approximately $\frac{3}{4}$–1 hour (depending on the size) at 170°C (325°F)/Gas 3, until tender. Remove the foil about halfway through the cooking time to brown them. Mix the cornflour with a little of the reserved apricot juice, then add the remaining juice and heat until thickened, stirring well. Place the thighs in a serving dish, decorate them with the reserved apricot halves and brush them with apricot juice glaze.

Cider-Braised Turkey Dumplings

2 turkey drumsticks
1 small onion
175 g (6 oz) pork sausagemeat
5 ml (1 teaspoon) ground
   coriander
2.5 ml ($\frac{1}{2}$ teaspoon) salt
pepper
25 g (1 oz) butter
1 small green pepper
1 small red pepper
25 g (1 oz) cornflour
250 ml ($\frac{1}{2}$ pint) dry cider
8 black olives

Remove the meat from the drumsticks, discarding skin and sinews. Mince the meat finely with the onion and mix it with the sausagemeat, coriander, salt and pepper. Shape this into 10 small balls and fry them in the butter until evenly browned. Drain the balls and now use the butter to soften the sliced peppers. Mix the cornflour with a little cider and then add the remaining cider. Put this into the pan with the peppers. Add the turkey balls and stoned olives, cover and simmer for 15 minutes. Serve with noodles or rice and a green salad.

Turkey Casserole with Dumplings

2 large turkey wings
15 g ($\frac{1}{2}$ oz) seasoned plain flour
25 g (1 oz) butter
1 medium onion
2 sticks celery
1 small green pepper
225-g (8-oz) can peeled
   tomatoes
1 can water (use the empty
   tomato tin)
salt and pepper
pinch of thyme

Parsley and Bacon
Dumplings:
15 g ($\frac{1}{2}$ oz) butter
25 g (1 oz) self-raising flour
salt
5 ml (1 teaspoon) chopped
   parsley
$\frac{1}{2}$ rasher bacon
12 ml (scant tablespoon) milk

Toss the wings in seasoned flour and fry them in the butter until lightly browned. Remove them from the pan. Add the remaining flour, stir and cook it until brown. Add the chopped onion, chopped celery and sliced green pepper and cook, stirring, for 3 minutes. Add the tomatoes, water, thyme and seasonings. Return the wings to the pan, cover with a lid and simmer for $\frac{3}{4}$–1 hour, or until almost cooked.

Make the dumplings by rubbing the butter into the sifted flour and salt, adding the other ingredients and mixing this into a soft dough. Form the dough into 4 balls, add them to the pan and simmer for 20 minutes.

Turkey Breasts in Orange and Walnut Sauce

oil for frying
4 turkey breasts
125 ml ($\frac{1}{4}$ pint) chicken stock
125 ml ($\frac{1}{4}$ pint orange juice
pinch of thyme
bayleaf
1 orange
10 ml (3 teaspoons) cornflour
30 ml (2 tablespoons) Cointreau
10 ml (2 teaspoons) redcurrant
   jelly
50 g (2 oz) chopped walnuts

Heat the oil and fry the turkey breasts until golden on both sides. Transfer them to a casserole and pour over the stock and ornage juice. Add seasoning and cook for 30 minutes at 180°C (350°F)/Gas 4. Pour off the juices and keep the turkey breasts warm. Mix the juice of the orange with the cornflour and add thin strips of orange rind, Cointreau, redcurrant jelly and the nuts. Stir this over a gentle heat until thickened, and then blend in the juices from the turkey breasts. Place the turkey breasts in a serving dish, pour over some of the sauce and serve the remaining sauce separately.

Spiced Apricot Turkey

4 fillets of turkey or 2 breasts,
    halved
salt and pepper
15 ml (1 tablespoon) oil
15 g (½ oz) butter
1 large onion
15 ml (1 tablespoon) tomato
    purée
30 ml (2 tablespoons) vinegar
45 ml (3 tablespoons) brown
    sugar
15 ml (1 tablespoon)
    Worcestershire sauce
45 ml (3 tablespoons) lemon
    juice
5 ml (1 teaspoon) paprika
175 ml (7 fl oz) water
75 g (3 oz) dried apricots
50 g (2 oz) sultanas or raisins
5 ml (1 teaspoon) cornflour
chopped parsley

Soak the apricots in cold water to cover overnight. Trim the turkey and season it lightly with salt and pepper. Heat the oil and butter in a pan and brown the turkey all over. Transfer it to an ovenware casserole. Fry the sliced onion in the same fat until it is just beginning to brown. Drain off all the fat from the pan and add the tomato purée, vinegar, sugar, Worcestershire sauce, lemon juice, paprika, 5 ml (1 teaspoon) salt and the water and bring this to the boil. Add the apricots and sultanas or raisins and simmer for 2 minutes. Pour this over the turkey, cover the pan with a lid or foil and cook at 180°C (350°F)/Gas 4 for ¾ hour, until tender. Remove any surplus fat from the juices and thicken them with the cornflour blended with a little cold water. Sprinkle with parsley and serve with boiled or creamed potatoes.

Turkey in a Pastry Case

2 450-g (1-lb) turkey breasts
175 g (6 oz) mushrooms
25 g (1 oz) onion
25 g (1 oz) butter
1 turkey liver
225 g (8 oz) sausagemeat
50 g (2 oz) fresh white
    breadcrumbs
30 ml (2 tablespoons) chopped
    parsley
salt and pepper
350 g (12 oz) puff pastry
1 egg

Skin the breasts and slice each breast across into two thinner pieces. Beat these out between sheets of grease-proof paper until quite thin. Finely chop the mushrooms and onions and fry them gently in the butter with the chopped liver, until quite dry. Stir in the sausage-meat and cook gently for 5 minutes. Add the bread-crumbs, parsley and seasoning. Roll out the pastry to about 30 cm (12 in) square. Place one turkey piece in the centre and pile the stuffing along its length. Spread the remaining meat over this, then wrap the pastry over to enclose it, sealing the edges with beaten egg. Place the parcel on a baking sheet, seam underneath, and decorate it with pastry trimmings. Glaze it with beaten egg. Bake it at 220°C (425°F)/Gas 7 for 20 minutes then reduce the temperature to 180°C (350°F)/Gas 4 for 35 minutes. Serve in slices, either hot or cold.

Turkeybabs

450 g (1 lb) turkey meat
12 mushrooms
4 small tomatoes
8 small onions
1 green pepper
bayleaves

Sauce:
90 ml (6 tablespoons) oil
15 ml (1 tablespoon) tomato
   purée
15 ml (1 tablespoon)
   Worcestershire sauce
1 small onion
60 ml (4 tablespoons) tomato
   ketchup
30 ml (2 tablespoons) wine
   vinegar
salt and pepper

Cut the turkey into 2.5 xm (1 in) cubes. Drop the mushrooms into boiling water and simmer them for 1 minute. Drain and thread them, with the other ingredients, on 4 skewers.

Mix together the ingredients for the sauce, chopping the onion finely. Brush this over the meat and vegetables, then grill them for 15–20 minutes, turning them frequently and brushing them with sauce until it is all used up. Serve the turkeybabs on the skewers on a bed of boiled rice.

Turkey Pot Roast Dinner

2 turkey thighs (approx 550 g
   (1¼ lb) each)
5 ml (1 teaspoon) salt
1 ml (¼ teaspoon) pepper
15 ml (1 tablespoon) oil
1 large onion
2 cloves garlic
1.2 ml (¼ teaspoon) basil
2.5 ml (½ teaspoon) thyme
5 ml (1 teaspoon) grated lemon
   rind
2 chicken stock cubes
250 ml (½ pint) water
4 medium potatoes
4 medium carrots
15 g (½ oz) cornflour
15 ml (1 tablespoon) chopped
   parsley

Use turkey thighs weighing about 550 g (1¼ lb) each. Season them with salt and pepper and brown them slowly in a little oil in a deep pan or iron casserole. Add the chopped onion, crushed garlic and (½ teaspoon) lemon peel, basil and thyme to the pan and fry it lightly. Dissolve the stock cubes in the water and pour this over the turkey and then heat this to boiling point. Reduce the heat, cover the pan and simmer for 1¾–2 hours, until the meat is tender. Add the peeled potatoes and sliced carrots for the last 20 minutes of cooking. When the vegetables and meat are tender, remove them to a heated serving dish. Skim off and discard any surface fat. Blend the cornflour with a tablespoon of cold water and stir it into the juices in the pan. Cook, stirring, until the mixture boils and thickens slightly. Spoon the sauce over the turkey and vegetables. Combine the remaining ½ teaspoon lemon peel with the parsley and sprinkle it over the turkey.

Using up a Turkey

One of the great joys of eating turkey is the anticipation of so many delicious meals still to come. Even a small bird can produce a wide range of meals, which makes turkey-buying a sensible economy. To start with, there is the carcase which yields valuable stock for soup and casseroles, and this can be made either from a fresh carcase which has had the joints removed, or from the remains of a roast bird. Cold turkey meat, both light and dark, is easily converted into casseroles, pies, curries and salads, and even the smallest leftover portions can be minced to make pâté or a sandwich spread.

A turkey has large giblets, and these can go into the stock to make gravy for a roast, and then to make soup. The giblets are lean meat and can be chopped or minced to mix with the turkey meat for second-day dishes, but the liver is always worth using separately. It will be enough to make an omelette for two people, or can be used like chicken liver to make pâté.

Turkey Soup

350 g (12 oz) cooked turkey
4 sticks celery
3 carrots
1 onion
1 small green pepper
25 g (1 oz) butter
25 g (1 oz) plain flour
625 ml (1¼ pints) stock
125 ml (¼ pint) milk
125 ml (¼ pint) single cream
salt and pepper
chopped parsley

Dice the turkey. Slice the celery, carrots, onion and pepper. Soften the vegetables in the butter, without letting them colour. Sprinkle in the flour, off the heat, and blend in the stock. Simmer this gently for 15 minutes until the vegetables are tender. Add the turkey and heat it through, and then add the milk and cream. Adjust the seasoning, reheat, and serve hot, sprinkled with parsley.

Grandma's Turkey Soup

½ turkey carcase
1.5 litres (3 pints) cold water
3 large leeks
50 g (2 oz) pearl barley
2 bayleaves
7.5 cm (3 in) cinnamon stick
salt and pepper
100 g (4 oz) cooked turkey
30 ml (2 tablespoons) chopped
    parsley

Break the carcase up roughly and put it in a large saucepan. Add the water and bring it slowly to the boil. Simmer for 2 hours. Skim any froth off the top and strain the stock into another pan. Bring it to the boil again and add the leeks, barley, bayleaves, cinnamon, salt and pepper. Cover the pan and simmer the soup for 1 hour. Remove the bayleaves and cinnamon stick and add the shredded turkey and parsley.

Cream of Turkey Soup

1 turkey carcase
turkey giblets
1 medium onion
1 bayleaf
pinch of ground nutmeg
salt and pepper
40 g (1½ oz) cornflour
250 ml (½ pint) milk
1 stick celery
10 ml (2 teaspoons) chopped
    tarragon
125 ml (¼ pint) single cream

This soup can be made from a raw turkey carcase from which the joints have been removed, or from a cooked leftover carcase. Put it into a pan with the giblets (the liver may be saved for an omelette or pâté), sliced onion, bayleaf, nutmeg, salt and pepper. Just cover with water, bring it to the boil and simmer for 45 minutes. Strain and keep the stock. Chop the giblets and meat from the bones. Put the bones back into the stock and continue boiling the stock to reduce it to 1 litre (2 pints). Strain the stock again and put it into a clean pan. Mix the cornflour with a little milk and then add this to the stock with the remaining milk. Add the finely chopped celery and simmer for 10 minutes. Stir in the chopped meat and tarragon and reheat this. Stir in the cream just before serving. Garnish the soup with cubes of fried or toasted bread.

Turkey Pâté

225 g (8 oz) cooked turkey
1 medium onion
1 hard-boiled egg
100 g (4 oz) mushrooms
few drops of Worcestershire
    sauce
125 ml (¼ pint) mayonnaise
15 ml (1 tablespoon) brandy

Mince the turkey, onion, egg and mushrooms coarsely. Mix them with the sauce, mayonnaise and brandy and press this into a container or four individual dishes. Serve with salad or hot toast.

133

Potted Turkey

450 g (1 lb) cooked turkey
giblets (including liver)
1 bayleaf
sprig of parsley
sprig of thyme
8 peppercorns
75 g (3 oz) butter
1 medium onion
15 ml (1 tablespoon) chopped
   sage
salt and pepper

Cut the cooked turkey into very small dice. Cook all the giblets, in water to cover, with the bayleaf, parsley, thyme and peppercorns for 1 hour. Drain and reserve the stock. Dice the liver and heart finely and mix them with the meat from the neck and the turkey meat. Chop the onion finely and soften it in the butter, until golden. Mix this with the meat, 250 ml ($\frac{1}{2}$ pint) stock, sage, and salt and pepper to taste. Put it into a serving dish, or eight individual dishes and chill them before serving. Serve with salad, or toast and butter.

Country Turkey Pie

275 g (10 oz) puff pastry
50 g (2 oz) butter or margarine
40 g (1½ oz) plain flour
   625 ml (1¼ pints) milk
1½ chicken stock cubes
salt
2.5 ml (½ teaspoon)
   Worcestershire sauce
22 ml (1½ tablespoons) dry
   sherry
3 drops of Tabasco sauce
175 g (6 oz) sliced fresh
   mushrooms
350 g (12 oz) cooked turkey
225 g (8 oz) cooked button or
   baby onions
175 g (6 oz) cooked carrots
15 ml (1 tablespoon) melted
   butter for glazing
15 ml (1 tablespoon) grated
   Parmesan cheese

Melt the butter and blend in the flour. Stir in the milk slowly and add the chicken stock cubes, salt and Worcestershire sauce. Cook, stirring, until the sauce boils and thickens. Stir in the sherry and Tabasco sauce. Add the cubed turkey meat, mushrooms, carrots and onions and heat this through. Turn the mixture into a pie dish and place the pastry over it, fluting the edges of the pastry against the rim.

Make a small hole in the centre of the pastry to allow steam to escape and decorate the pie, if liked. Bake at 200°C (400°F)/Gas 6 for about 20 minutes, until the pastry is almost done. Brush the top of the pie with melted butter and sprinkle it with the cheese. Bake the pie for 10 minutes longer, until browned.

Old English Turkey Pie

1 packet sage and onion stuffing
25 g (1 oz) butter
100 g (4 oz) chipolata sausages
15 g (½ oz) plain flour
250 ml (¼ pint) turkey stock
salt and pepper
175 g (6 oz) cooked turkey
225 g (8 oz) puff pastry

Prepare the stuffing as directed on the packet. Divide and shape the mixture into 8 balls. Fry the balls and chopped sausages in melted butter until golden, remove and place them in a fairly deep pie dish. Stir the flour into the remaining butter and cook for 1 minute. Gradually blend in the stock. Bring this to the boil, stirring well. Season with salt and pepper. Add the diced turkey to the sauce and pour it over the stuffing balls and sausages. Roll out the pastry and cover the pie. Brush the pastry with a little beaten egg and bake the pie at 220°C (425°F)/Gas 7 for 30 minutes.

Turkey Orange Pie

450 g (1 lb) cooked turkey
225 g (8 oz) sausagemeat
25 g (1 oz) breadcrumbs
grated rind of 1 orange
5 ml (1 teaspoon) mixed herbs
5 ml (1 teaspoon) chopped
   parsley
salt and pepper
1 egg
a little oil
15 g (½ oz) butter
15 g (½ oz) plain flour
250 ml (¼ pint) stock
1 orange
15 ml (1 tablespoon) brandy
450 g (1 lb) mashed potato

Dice the turkey. Combine the sausagemeat, breadcrumbs, grated orange rind, herbs and seasoning together and pound this until it is well mixed. Add a beaten egg to bind the mixture. Roll this forcemeat into small balls about 2.4 cm (1 in) in diameter. Fry these until golden in a little oil, then drain and put them to one side. Melt the butter, stir in the flour and cook gently for 1 minute. Blend in the stock, then thicken it over the heat. Season. Take the rind off the orange with a potato peeler and cut it into needle-sized shreds. Squeeze the juice from the orange and add this to the sauce with the brandy. Combine the turkey, forcemeat balls and sauce. Pile this into an ovenware dish. Pipe mashed potato around the edge and bake the pie at 180°C (350°F)/Gas 4 for 20–30 minutes, until the potato is golden brown. Before serving, sprinkle with the orange shreds.

Turkey Curry Pie

350 g (12 oz) cooked turkey
1 medium onion
1 cooking apple
25 g (1 oz) butter
5 ml (1 teaspoon) curry paste
25 g (1 oz) plain flour
salt and pepper
pinch of ground ginger
125 ml (¼ pint) stock
125 ml (¼ pint) milk
50 g (2 oz) mushrooms
30 ml (2 tablespoons) single
  cream
1 hard-boiled egg
225 g (8 oz) shortcrust pastry
egg or milk for glazing

Cut the turkey into neat cubes. Chop the onion and apple and cook them in the butter until soft and golden. Stir in the curry paste, flour, salt, pepper and ginger and cook this for 2 minutes. Add the stock and milk and bring it to the boil. Add the turkey and sliced mushrooms and simmer for 15 minutes. Take the pan off the heat and stir in the cream. Add slices of egg and put the mixture into a pie dish. Cover this with pastry and brush it with a little beaten egg or milk. Bake at 200°C (400°F)/Gas 6 for 25 minutes.

Turkey Quiche

225 g (8 oz) shortcrust pastry
175 g (6 oz) cooked turkey
1 red pepper
1 green pepper
2 eggs
1 egg yolk
250 ml (½ pint) milk
125 ml (¼ pint) single cream
salt and pepper

Roll out the pastry and line a 17.5-cm (7-in) flan ring. Cut the turkey into chunks. Dice the peppers. Mix together the eggs, milk, cream, and seasonings. Sprinkle the turkey and pepper over the bottom of the pastry. Pour on the egg mixture and bake the quiche at 180°C (350°F)/Gas 4 for 25–30 minutes, until firm and golden.

Turkey Flan

275 g (10 oz) shortcrust pastry
1 small onion
25 g (1 oz) butter
50 g (2 oz) button mushrooms
100 g (4 oz) cooked turkey
2 tomatoes
2 eggs
125 ml (¼ pint) milk
75 g (3 oz) grated cheese
salt and pepper

Use pastry to line a 20-cm (8-in) flan ring. Fry the chopped onion in butter until soft and golden. Add the sliced mushrooms, chopped turkey and peeled tomatoes and cook for 5 minutes. Mix the eggs, milk, cheese and seasonings. Stir in the onion mixture and then pour the mixture into the flan. Bake at 200°C (400°F)/Gas 6 for 35 minutes until well risen and golden brown.

Marie Teresa Turkey

4 good slices of cooked turkey
　breast
stuffing from turkey
4 thin slices cooked ham
100 g (4 oz) mushrooms
375 ml (¾ pint) milk
25 g (1 oz) butter or margarine
25 g (1 oz) plain flour
salt and pepper
40 g (1½ oz) grated cheese

Spread each slice of turkey with a generous helping of stuffing and wrap it in a slice of cooked ham. Arrange these in a fairly shallow, greased, ovenware dish. Trim, wash and dry the mushrooms. Reserve 4, removing the stalks, and place them on the turkey bundles. Slice the remaining mushrooms, put them into a pan with the milk and bring this slowly to the boil. Cool and then strain. Melt the butter or margarine and work in the flour and milk. Bring this to the boil, season and add the mushrooms. Pour this carefully over the turkey. Sprinkle it evenly with the cheese and bake it at 200°C (400°F)/Gas 6 for 15 minutes. If necessary, put the dish under a hot grill to brown the surface. Serve with halved tomatoes, sprinkled with herbs and baked in the oven with the main dish, and a green salad.

Tropical Turkey Curry

1 medium onion
50 g (2 oz) butter
15 g (½ oz) plain flour
15 ml (1 tablespoon) hot curry
　powder
5 ml (1 teaspoon) ground
　coriander
5 ml (1 teaspoon) ground ginger
1 lemon
500 ml (1 pint) turkey stock
1 large ripe mango
1 small can pineapple chunks
350 g (12 oz) cooked turkey
75 ml (3 fl oz) double cream
salt

Peel and chop the onion. Fry it fairly quickly in the butter melted in a thick-bottomed frying pan. Stir in the flour, curry powder, coriander, ginger, grated lemon rind and juice. Cook this mixture gently for 5 minutes, stirring constantly. Carefully add the turkey stock, cover the pan and simmer for 30 minutes. Peel and roughly chop the mango. Drain the pineapple chunks, and cut up the pieces if necessary. Mix the fruit and chopped turkey into the sauce. Stir in the cream and add a little salt to taste. Serve the curry with saffron rice, crispy fried onions, chopped cucumber, chopped tomato, chopped hard-boiled egg, lemon wedges and poppadums.

Sweet and Sour Turkey

30 ml (2 tablespoons) soy sauce
15 ml (1 tablespoon) wine
  vinegar
10 ml (2 teaspoons)
  Worcestershire sauce
15 g (½ oz) cornflour
1 small can pineapple cubes
225 g (8 oz) ham
½ cucumber
4 sticks celery
2 tomatoes
salt and pepper
450 g (1 lb) cooked turkey meat

Blend together soy sauce, vinegar, Worcestershire sauce and cornflour. Drain the pineapple and heat the juice, made up to 500 ml (1 pint) with water. Pour this over the cornflour mixture and stir until smooth. Return this to the pan and bring it to the boil, stirring until it thickens. Add the diced ham and pineapple. Cut the cucumber and celery into narrow strips. Add these to sauce and season with salt and pepper. Simmer gently for 20 minutes. Add the diced turkey meat, heat it through and serve with boiled rice.

Turkey Leftover Pie

cold turkey
poultry stuffing
gravy
bacon rolls
sausages

After a turkey meal, there are often a lot of items left over, but this delicious dish can solve the problem. It turns out rather like a pâté and may be served hot, with leftover gravy and cranberry sauce, or cold, in slices with salad, or in sandwiches.

Cut white and dark meat into small pieces, and use any of the odd pieces which do not look attractive enough to serve on their own. Use leftover stuffing or stuffing balls, or make up a fresh quantity. Cut the sausages lengthwise in halves or thirds, and chop the cooked bacon rolls into small pieces. Line a shallow casserole or cake tin with stuffing and fill it with pieces of turkey, sausage, bacon and any stuffing balls. Moisten the whole with gravy and cover the mixture with a lid of stuffing. If you have a lot of stuffing, an extra layer can be placed in the middle. Brush this with a little fat and bake it at 180°C (350°F)/Gas 4 for 1 hour. Serve hot, or press under weights in a cold place and later serve cold.

Cold Curried Turkey

350 g (12 oz) cooked turkey
75 ml (5 tablespoons)
  mayonnaise
15 ml (1 tablespoon) single
  cream
15 g (½ oz) curry powder
1 small tin apricots
chopped walnuts
salt and pepper

Garnish:
tomatoes
black olives
watercress
paprika

Cut the turkey into small pieces. Mix the mayonnaise, cream, curry powder, sieved apricots, walnuts and seasoning. Spoon this sauce over the turkey and leave it to stand in a cold place for a few hours before serving. Garnish the dish with tomatoes, olives and watercress and dust the top with paprika. Serve with a green salad.

Turkey Roll

350 g (12 oz) cooked turkey
225 g (8 oz) cooked ham
1 small onion
salt and pepper
pinch of ground nutmeg
2.5 ml (½ teaspoon) mixed herbs
1 large egg
dried breadcrumbs

Mince the turkey, ham and onion finely. Season it well with salt, pepper, nutmeg and herbs and bind it all together with the egg. Put into a greased bowl or stone marmalade jar, cover with foil and put into a saucepan. Pour in boiling water to come half-way up the container, and steam for 1 hour, topping up with a little more boiling water if necessary. Leave in the container for 15 minutes, then turn out and coat in a thin layer of breadcrumbs. Cool completely and serve sliced with salad or in sandwiches.

Turkey Cakes

450 g (1 lb) cooked turkey
225 g (8 oz) cooked potatoes
125 ml (¼ pint) gravy
5 ml (1 teaspoon) tomato purée
salt and pepper
10 ml (2 teaspoons) chopped
  parsley
flour or breadcrumbs

Mince the turkey finely and mix it with the mashed potatoes, gravy and tomato purée. Season well and add the parsley. Form the mixture into 12 flat cakes and coat them lightly in flour or breadcrumbs. Fry these on both sides until golden. Serve hot with vegetables, some grilled bacon and extra gravy.

139

Hot Turkey Salad

350 g (12 oz) cooked turkey
175 g (6 oz) celery
125 ml (¼ pint) mayonnaise
50 g (2 oz) toasted almonds
22 ml (1½ tablespoons) lemon
    juice
10 ml (2 teaspoons) grated
    onion
2.5 ml (½ teaspoon) salt
50 g (2 oz) grated cheese
2 small packets potato crisps

Cube the turkey, slice the celery and chop the almonds. Combine all the ingredients, except the cheese and potato crisps, and toss them with the mayonnaise until well mixed. Pile this into individual ovenware dishes and sprinkle the top of each with a mixture of grated cheese and crushed potato crisps. Bake at 230°C (450°F)/Gas 8 for 10 minutes.

Turkey and Grapefruit Salad

225 g (8 oz) cooked turkey meat
30 ml (2 tablespoons)
    mayonnaise
5 ml (1 teaspoon) lemon juice
30 ml (2 tablespoons) chopped
    mint
2 grapefruit
salt and pepper

Cut the cooked turkey into cubes. Mix together the mayonnaise, lemon juice and mint, and stir in the meat. Cut the grapefruit in half. Cut the pulp away from the pith and skin and add this to the turkey mixture. Season it wll and fill the grapefruit shells with the turkey mixture.

Toasted Turkey Sandwiches

4 large slices bread
chutney
50 g (2 oz) grated cheese
100 g (4 oz) cooked turkey
butter
button mushrooms
watercress

Spread each slice of bread with chutney and sprinkle them with the cheese. Cover 2 slices with the thinly sliced turkey and top them with the remaining bread slices. Butter the top of each sandwich and toast them under the grill. Turn them over, spread the new tops with butter and toast them again. Cut each sandwich into 4 triangles, place these on a heated dish and garnish it with the small mushrooms cooked in a little butter with sprigs of watercress.

140

Melon Boats

1 melon
225 g (8 oz) cooked turkey
2 sticks celery
2 oranges
walnut halves

Dressing:
yoghurt
30 ml (2 tablespoons) sherry
10 ml (2 teaspoons)
   Worcestershire sauce
2.5 ml ($\frac{1}{2}$ teaspoon) paprika
pinch of salt
few drops of Tabasco sauce
juice from the oranges

Peel the oranges and divide it into segments, saving any spilled juice for the dressing. Cut the melon in three and discard the seeds. Scoop out the flesh and cut it into large dice. Mix this with the turkey cut into bite-sized pieces, the celery and oranges and place this in the melon shells. Garnish the tops with walnut halves. Mix all the ingredients for the dressing and serve this separately.

Using Up the Bird

A chicken or turkey can always provide more than just one hot meal and perhaps a chicken salad. Even a few scraps of flesh can be turned into a second-day hot dish, and the final remains used to make a topping for toast, a sandwich, or a spread. The giblets should not be discarded. They can, of course, be used to make stock, and afterwards the lean meat of the giblets can be added to dishes or used on their own. Chicken livers also make tasty dishes, and while a single liver can be extended to make an omelette for two people or a savoury toast topping, it is worth saving a few livers in the refrigerator or freezer to make a family meal. The recipes in this section can be used for chicken or turkey leftovers.

Devilled Chicken

pieces of cooked chicken
5 ml (1 teaspoon) mustard
 powder
5 ml (1 teaspoon)
 Worcestershire sauce
5 ml (1 teaspoon) chutney
2.5 ml (½ teaspoon) curry
 powder
5 ml (1 teaspoon) tomato sauce
10 ml (2 teaspoons) vinegar
pinch of Cayenne pepper
pinch of sugar
25 g (1 oz) butter

Use large pieces of leg or breast meat, chicken wings or small drumsticks for this dish. Put the chicken pieces into an ovenware dish. Put all the other ingredients into a small thick-bottomed pan and bring them to the boil, stirring well. Pour this over the chicken and cook at 180°C (350°F)/Gas 4 for 10 minutes, turning once. Remove the pieces of chicken from the dish and grill them for 3 minutes on each side. Serve very hot with green salad and crusty bread.

White Devil

450 g (1 lb) cooked chicken
5 ml (1 teaspoon) French
   mustard
5 ml (1 teaspoon) chutney
15 ml (1 tablespoon)
   Worcestershire sauce
salt and pepper
250 ml (½ pint) double cream

Cut the chicken in large pieces and arrange them in a shallow fireproof dish. Mix the mustard, chutney, sauce, salt and pepper. Whip the cream to soft peaks and add the sauce mixture. Pour this over the chicken and bake at 190°C (375°F)/Gas 5 for 20 minutes.

American Festival Chicken

50 g (2 oz) butter
1 large onion
100 g (4 oz) cooked ham
5 ml (1 teaspoon) curry powder
15 g (½ oz) plain flour
225 g (8 oz) button mushrooms
250 ml (½ pint) chicken stock
125 ml (¼ pint) double cream
50 ml (2 fl oz) canned pineapple
   juice
15 ml (1 tablespoon) lemon juice
pinch of salt
350 g (12 oz) cooked chicken

Melt the butter and cook the chopped onion and diced ham until the onion is soft and golden. Stir in the curry powder, flour and thinly sliced mushrooms. Add the chicken stock and cream, stir well, and simmer for 10 minutes. Add the pineapple juice, lemon juice and salt to taste and then the cubed chicken. Heat these together for 10 minutes and serve over cooked rice. In America this is often served in scooped-out pineapple halves with rice in the bottom of each pineapple shell and with a garnish of toasted flaked coconut.

Chicken Parmesan

450 g (1 lb) cold chicken
seasoned flour
1 egg
50 g (2 oz) grated Parmesan
   cheese
25 g (1 oz) dry breadcrumbs

Cut the chicken into large thick pieces. Dip these in seasoned flour and then in beaten egg. Mix the cheese and breadcrumbs and coat the chicken pieces with this mixture. Grill them under a medium grill until hot right through, and serve with grilled tomatoes and a green salad. This cheese and breadcrumb coating may also be used for chicken joints which are to be fried, and gives a most delicious flavour.

143

Chicken Rarebit

25 g (1 oz) butter
50 g (2 oz) mushrooms
25 g (1 oz) plain flour
pinch of cayenne pepper
5 ml (1 teaspoon) made mustard
salt
250 ml (½ pint) milk
225 g (8 oz) cooked chicken
4 slices buttered toast
50 g (2 oz) grated cheese

Melt the butter and cook the chopped mushrooms for 2 minutes. Stir in the flour and cook for 1 minute. Add the cayenne pepper, mustard and salt. Stir in the milk gradually and bring it to the boil, stirring all the time. Add the mushrooms and chopped chicken and simmer for 3 minutes. Spread this mixture on the toast, sprinkle it with cheese, and brown it under a hot grill.

Chicken Macaroni

175 g (6 oz) short-cut macaroni
3 rashers streaky bacon
100 g (4 oz) mushrooms
25 g (1 oz) butter
225 g (8 oz) cooked chicken
3 tomatoes
250 ml (½ pint) white sauce
100 g (4 oz) grated cheese

Cook the macaroni in boiling salted water until tender. Drain and put it into a casserole. Chop the bacon and slice the mushrooms and cook them in the butter until soft and golden. Put these on top of the macaroni. Cover this with the chopped chicken and top it with skinned and sliced tomatoes. Stir half the cheese into the sauce and pour it over the top. Sprinkle this with the remaining cheese and bake at 180°C (350°F)/Gas 4 for 25 minutes.

Chicken Tetrazzini

450 g (1 lb) cooked chicken
175 g (6 oz) spaghetti
225 g (8 oz) button mushrooms
50 g (2 oz) butter
25 g (1 oz) plain flour
250 ml (½ pint) chicken stock
125 ml (¼ pint) creamy milk
salt and pepper
pinch of ground nutmeg
60 ml (4 tablespoons) sherry
75 g (3 oz) grated cheese

Cut the chicken into small thin strips. Cook the spaghetti in boiling salted water, until tender, and drain it thoroughly. Slice the mushrooms thinly and cook them in half the butter. Melt the remaining butter, work in the flour and gradually add the stock. Bring this back to the boil, stir in the creamy milk and cook gently for 10 minutes. Season with salt, pepper, nutmeg and sherry and stir in the cheese, reserving a little for the topping. Moisten the chicken with a little of the sauce. Mix the spaghetti and mushrooms and arrange them in a circle in an ovenware dish. Put the chicken in the centre. Sprinkle this with the reserved cheese and bake it at 190°C (375°F)/Gas 5 for 20 minutes.

Chicken a la King

450 g (1 lb) cooked chicken
50 g (2 oz) butter
1 green pepper
100 g (4 oz) button mushrooms
25 g (1 oz) plain flour
250 ml (½ pint) chicken stock
125 ml (¼ pint) milk
salt and pepper
15 ml (1 tablespoon) dry sherry
125 ml (¼ pint) single cream
2 egg yolks

Cut the chicken into neat pieces. Melt the butter and cook the thinly sliced pepper for 5 minutes, until soft. Slice the mushrooms and cook them for 3 minutes. Work in the flour and then gradually stir in the stock and milk. Stir this over a low heat to make a creamy sauce. Season with salt and pepper. Add the pieces of chicken and the sherry and heat through. Stir together the cream and egg yolks and add this to the sauce. Heat gently, but do not boil. Serve with rice. This also makes a delicious filling for vol-au-vent cases.

Chicken and Spinach Cream

350 g (12 oz) cooked chicken
1 chicken liver
1 small onion
100 g (4 oz) spinach purée
    (frozen)
50 g (2 oz) cottage cheese
2 eggs
salt and pepper
pinch of nutmeg
25 g (1 oz) Parmesan cheese

Cut the chicken in small pieces. Chop the chicken liver and onion. Thaw the spinach until just soft. Put all the ingredients, except the Parmesan cheese, into a liquidizer and blend until well mixed. Put the mixture into a greased ovenware dish and sprinkle it with cheese. Put the dish into a roasting tin of water and bake at 180°C (350°F)/Gas 4 for 1 hour. Serve hot with vegetables or a salad, and crusty bread.

Chicken Soufflé

225 g (8 oz) cooked chicken
25 g (1 oz) butter
25 g (1 oz) plain flour
125 ml (¼ pint) chicken stock
salt and pepper
5 ml (1 teaspoon) lemon juice
5 ml (1 teaspoon) anchovy
    essence
3 eggs
1 tablespoon single cream

Shred the chicken finely. Mel the butter and stir in the flour. Cook this for 1 minute and then slowly stir in the stock. Simmer for 5 minutes, stirring well, and then cool. Add the chicken, seasonings, lemon juice and anchovy essence. Separate the eggs. Stir the egg yolks and the single cream into the chicken mixture. Fold in the stiffly beaten egg whites and put the whole into a greased 15 cm (6 in) soufflé dish. Bake at 200°C (400°F)/Gas 6 for 35 minutes, until well risen and firm to the touch. Serve at once with a crisp salad.

145

Chicken Pilaff

225 g (8 oz) long-grain rice
1 medium onion
1 clove garlic
40 g (1½ oz) turkey dripping or
    butter
1 bayleaf
salt and pepper
100 g (4 oz) mushrooms
500 ml (1 pint) chicken stock
350 g (12 oz) cooked chicken
25 g (1 oz) grated cheese

Wash the rice and drain it well. Chop the onion and garlic finely. Melt the fat and cook the rice, onion and garlic until the rice looks transparent and the onion is soft and golden. Add the bayleaf, seasoning and chopped mushrooms and stir well. Pour on the hot stock and simmer for 10 minutes. Stir in the chopped chicken and continue cooking for about 10 minutes until the stock has been absorbed and the rice is tender. Remove the bayleaf and serve the dish with grated cheese.

Little Chicken Patties

225 g (8 oz cooked chicken
100 g (4 oz) fresh white
    breadcrumbs
10 ml (2 teaspoons)
    Worcestershire sauce
salt and pepper
2 eggs
a few dry breadcrumbs

Mince the chicken finely and mix it with the breadcrumbs, Worcestershire sauce, salt, pepper and eggs. If you have any cold gravy left from serving the chicken, use a little to bind the mixture. Shape the mixture into eight flat cakes. Dust them with the dry breadcrumbs and fry them in fat or oil until golden on both sides. Serve these hot with vegetables or cold with salad, or use them to fill soft baps for a picnic.

Chicken Croquettes

350 g (12 oz) cooked chicken
25 g (1 oz) butter
25 g (1 oz) plain flour
125 ml (¼ pint) chicken stock or
    milk
50 g (2 oz) mushrooms
salt and pepper
5 ml (1 teaspoon) chopped
    parsley
1 egg
breadcrumbs

Mince the chicken finely. Melt the butter and work in the flour. Cook this for 1 minute and then gradually work in the liquid, stirring well. Add the chopped mushrooms, salt, pepper and parsley, and cook for 3 minutes. Stir in the chicken, mix it well and turn it out onto a plate to cool. Divide the mixture into 12 equal-sized pieces and roll them into sausage shapes. Dip them in beaten egg and breadcrumbs and then fry them until golden. Serve hot with vegetables, or cold with salad.

Chicken and Orange Pancakes

100 g (4 oz) plain flour
pinch of salt
1 egg
250 ml (½ pint) milk
2 oranges
40 g (1½ oz) butter or
*   margarine*
1 onion
60 ml (4 tablespoons) white
*   wine*
125 ml (¼ pint) chicken stock
salt and pepper
225 g (8 oz) cooked chicken
10 ml (2 teaspoons) cornflour
15 ml (1 tablespoon) chopped
*   parsley*

Make a batter with the flour, salt, egg and milk. Add the grated rind of 1 orange to the pancake batter and fry 8 pancakes. Stack these on a plate and keep them warm. Melt the butter in a pan and fry the chopped onion gently until soft, but not coloured. Add the grated rind of the remaining orange and the juice of both oranges, the wine, stock and seasonings. Bring to the boil, cover and simmer for 5 minutes. Add the diced chicken and continue cooking for 5 minutes. Blend the cornflour in a little cold water and add it to the pan. Return the liquid to the boil for 2 minutes. Adjust the seasonings, stir in the parsley and then use this to fill the pancakes and then roll them up. Place them in a warmed and lightly greased shallow, ovenware dish and cover it with foil. Cook at 180°C (350°F)/Gas 4 for 20 minutes.

Maryland Fritters

25 g (1 oz) butter
25 g (1 oz) plain flour
250 ml (½ pint) milk
175 g (6 oz) cooked chicken
200 g (7 oz) canned sweetcorn
1 medium onion
2.5 ml (½ teaspoon) mustard
*   powder*
15 ml (1 tablespoon) chopped
*   parsley*
2.5 ml (½ teaspoon) salt
pepper

Batter:
125 ml (¼ pint) beer
60 ml (4 tablespoons) water
175 g (6 oz) plain flour
1.2 ml (¼ teaspoon) salt
oil for frying

Melt the butter in a pan, stir in the flour and cook for 1 minute, stirring well. Remove the pan from the heat and gradually stir in the milk. Cook this over a low heat, stirring, until the sauce thickens, and then cool. Stir in the chicken, drained corn, chopped onion, mustard, parsley and seasoning. Shape into 8 oblongs about 7.5 × 5 cm (3 × 2 in) on a well-floured surface.

Make the batter just before cooking. To make the batter, mix the flour and salt. Add half the beer and beat well. Beat in the remaining beer and water. Coat the fritters in batter and shallow-fry in oil until golden brown. Serve them with grilled tomatoes or a green salad. For a more substantial meal, add sausages, bacon or fried eggs.

Crisp Chicken Balls

50 g (2 oz) rashers streaky
  bacon
1 small onion
50 g (2 oz) mushrooms
225 g (8 oz) cooked chicken
5 g (2 oz) butter
50 g (2 oz) plain flour
125 ml (¼ pint) chicken stock
125 ml (¼ pint) milk
2.5 ml (½ teaspoon) made
  mustard
salt and pepper
5 ml (1 teaspoon) chopped
  parsley
25 g (1 oz) plain flour
1 egg
dried breadcrumbs

Fry the bacon until cooked but not crisp. Remove it from the pan and use the bacon fat to fry the finely chopped onion and mushrooms, until tender. Mince the bacon and chicken. Melt the butter and stir in the flour. Add the stock and milk and bring this to the boil, stirring all the time. Simmer for 2 minutes. Add the chicken and bacon, mustard, salt, pepper, parsley, onion and mushrooms. Mix well and leave it to cool. Form this mixture into 8 balls and roll them in the flour. Dip them into the beaten egg and coat them with breadcrumbs. Deep-fry them in hot fat until golden. Serve with chutney.

Savoury Chicken Livers

225 g (8 oz) chicken livers
4 rashers unsmoked bacon
1 medium onion
1 green pepper
2 tomatoes
25 g (1 oz) butter
15 g (½ oz) plain flour
125 ml (¼ pint) stock
salt and pepper
15 ml (1 tablespoon) whisky or
  sherry

Cut each liver in four pieces. Cut the bacon into strips. Put the bacon into a frying pan and heat it until the fat runs. Add the thinly sliced onion and cook it until soft and golden. Stir in 4 tablespoons hot water. Add the thinly sliced green pepper. Skin the tomatoes and remove the seeds. Chop the flesh and add this to the pan. Cover the pan and cook over low heat for 5 minutes. Push this mixture to the side of the pan. Put the butter into the pan and cook the livers until coloured on the outside, but still pink within. Work in the flour and stock (this can be giblet or chicken stock), stir the livers into the other ingredients, and simmer this until thick and creamy. Season with salt and pepper and stir in the whisky or sherry. Serve this on a bed of rice or pasta. A crushed garlic clove or a few button mushrooms may be added if liked.

Chicken Liver Kebabs (1)

100 g (4 oz) chicken livers
4 rashers lean bacon
8 small mushrooms
4 small tomatoes
salt and pepper
10 ml (2 teaspoons) mixed herbs
15 ml (1 tablespoon) oil

Cut each liver into three or four pieces. Cut the bacon rashers in squares. Cut the tomatoes in half. Thread the liver, bacon, mushrooms and tomatoes onto four smooth skewers. Season these lightly and sprinkle them with herbs. Brush the kebabs with oil and grill them under a medium heat for 6 minutes, turning once or twice. Serve with rice or crusty bread.

Devilled Poultry Livers

poultry livers
butter
salt and pepper
pinch of mustard powder
Worcestershire sauce or
  mushroom ketchup
buttered toast

A single turkey or goose liver will serve two or three people, but 2 or 3 chicken or duck livers will be needed. Cook the livers lightly in a little butter so the outside becomes brown but the inside remains pink and slightly underdone. Mash the livers with the juices left in the pan and season well with salt, pepper, mustard, sauce or ketchup. Spread this on toast and serve very hot.

Savoury Yorkshire Puddings

65 g (2½ oz) plain flour
salt and pepper
1 egg
125 ml (¼ pint) milk
1 small onion
225 g (8 oz) chicken livers
25 g (1 oz) butter
2.5 ml (½ teaspoon)
  Worcestershire sauce

Beat together 50 g (2 oz) flour with seasoning, egg and milk to make a creamy batter. Leave to stand for 30 minutes. Meanwhile, chop the onion finely. Cut each chicken liver in four pieces and toss these in the remaining flour. Melt the butter and cook it until soft and golden. Stir in the liver pieces and cook them until the outsides are coloured, but the insides remain pink. Add the sauce and stir well. Put a little oil or dripping into 12 tart tins and heat them at 220°C (425°F)/Gas 7 for 3 minutes. Pour butter into each tin, working quickly, and sprinkle the liver and onion mixture on top. Return the tin to the oven and cook for 8 minutes until the puddings are crisp and golden. Serve at once with roast chicken. I like to put a little chopped fresh sage into the liver mixture sometimes.

Giblet Dumplings

1 set chicken giblets
1 litre (2 pints) water
50 g (2 oz) butter
50 g (2 oz) plain flour
100 g (4 oz) breadcrumbs
1 egg
15 ml (1 tablespoon) chopped
* parsley*
salt and pepper

Clean the giblets and cook them in the water until tender. Cool slightly and drain them, reserving the stock. Chop the giblets in small pieces and mix these with the softened butter, flour, breadcrumbs, egg, parsley and seasoning. Moisten this with a little stock to make a soft but firm mixture. Form this into small balls and chill for 1 hour. Drop the balls into hot soup or a casserole, to cook for 15 minutes before serving. The remaining stock can be used in making the soup or casserole.

Chicken Liver Omelette

1 chicken liver
2 rashers streaky bacon
1 small onion
50 g (2 oz) mushrooms
3 eggs
salt and pepper
25 g (1 oz) butter

Cut the chicken liver into small pieces. Chop the bacon and put it into an omelette pan or small frying pan. Heat it gently until the bacon begins to get crisp and the fat runs out. Stir in the liver and the finely chopped onion. Add the chopped mushrooms and cook gently until the vegetables are soft. Beat the eggs lightly and season them well with salt and pepper. Drain off any excess fat from the pan. Add the butter to the other ingredients and when it has melted, stir in the eggs. Stir and lift the mixture with a fork until just set. Fold it over once and serve on hot plates with salad and crusty bread. This omelette will serve 2 people. A little chopped green pepper may be added at the same time as the mushrooms.

Chicken Liver Kebabs (2)

350 g (12 oz) chicken livers
2 tomatoes
1 medium onion
50 g (2 oz) mushrooms
1 green pepper
4 bayleaves
125 ml (¼ pint) chicken stock
10 ml (2 teaspoons) vinegar
1 teaspoon Worcestershire sauce

Cut the tomatoes in half, and the onion in quarters. Leave the mushrooms whole and cut the green pepper in cubes. Arrane these ingredients on 4 skewers. Combine the stock, vinegar and sauce. Grill the kebabs for 20 minutes, turning occasionally. Serve on a bed of rice with a green salad.

Savoury Toast

1 set chicken giblets
100 g (4 oz) cooked drumstick
  meat
175 ml (7 fl oz) giblet stock
salt and pepper
5 ml (1 teaspoon)
  Worcestershire sauce
1 bacon rasher
buttered toast

Clean and cut up the giblets and simmer them in water to cover until tender. Use this stock for gravy to serve with the rest of the bird, but reserve 175 ml (7 fl oz) for this dish. Mince the cooked giblets with drumstick meat and moisten this with the stock. Season with salt, pepper and Worcestershire sauce and simmer for 5 minutes. Meanwhile grill the bacon until crisp and then crumble it into small pieces. Serve the chicken mixture on buttered toast, sprinkled with bacon pieces.

Chicken Livers on Toast

50 g (2 oz) bacon
75 g (3 oz) chicken livers
a little plain flour
50 g (2 oz) button mushrooms
salt and pepper
30 ml (2 tablespoons) dry sherry
2.5 ml (½ teaspoon)
  Worcestershire sauce
toast

Chop the bacon coarsely and heat it in a thick-bottomed pan until the fat runs. Wash and dry the livers and toss them in a little flour. Cook them with the bacon, tossing the pan over the heat until they are golden, and season with salt and pepper to taste. Add the thinly sliced mushrooms and stir over the heat until the mushrooms are tender. Take off the heat and stir in the sherry and Worcestershire sauce. Serve on hot toast. If preferred, serve with rice.

Chicken Horseradish Sandwich

175 ml (7 fl oz) mayonnaise
60 ml (4 tablespoons)
  horseradish sauce
350 g (12 oz) cooked chicken
3 large tomatoes
1 lettuce heart
salt and pepper
12 slices brown bread
butter

Mix the mayonnaise and horseradish sauce. Cut the chicken into neat strips. Slice the tomatoes across in thin slices, and chop the lettuce heart into thin strips. Butter 8 bread slices on one side only, and the remaining 4 slices on both sides. Arrange the chicken pieces on four of the bread slices and top them liberally with horse-radish mayonnaise. Top this with the four double-buttered bread slices. Put a little more horseradish mayonnaise on top of this and then the tomato slices and lettuce. Season well with salt and pepper. Top with the remaining bread slices and press them down firmly. Cut each sandwich in four pieces to serve.

French-Toasted Chicken Sandwich

225 g (8 oz) cooked chicken
1 stick celery
15 ml (1 tablespoon) chopped
    parsley
15 ml (1 tablespoon) apple
    chutney
15 ml (1 tablespoon)
    mayonnaise
salt and pepper
12 thin bread slices
3 eggs
90 ml (6 tablespoons) milk
    butter or oil for frying

Mince together the chicken and celery. Mix this with the parsley, chutney, mayonnaise and seasoning. Make 6 sandwiches using this filling and some unbuttered bread. Beat the eggs and milk together and season it lightly. Dip each sandwich into the egg mixture, coating each side. Heat the butter or oil and gently fry the sandwiches on both sides until the filling is thoroughly heated and the sandwiches are golden brown. Serve hot with chutney and a salad.

Chicken and Ham Paste

225 g (8 oz) cooked chicken
40 g (1½ oz) cooked ham or
    bacon
50 g (2 oz) butter
salt and pepper
pinch of ground nutmeg

Cut the chicken and ham or bacon in small pieces and put them through a fine mincer *twice*. Mash this well in a basin until the mixture is smooth. Soften the butter, but do not melt it. Work this butter into the chicken and ham mixture with plenty of salt, pepper and nutmeg. Put this into a pot and press it down firmly. Chill well and store it in the referigerator. Use the paste in slices with salad, as a sandwich filling, or on toast.

Chicken Sandwich Spread

175 g (6 oz) cooked chicken
60 ml (4 tablespoons)
    mayonnaise
15 ml (1 tablespoon) chutney
salt and pepper
2.5 ml (½ teaspoon) vinegar

Cut the chicken into small pieces. Put the remaining ingredients into a blender and blend on a low speed for 10 seconds. Add the chicken and continue blending until it is all finely chopped. If a blender is not available, mince the chicken finely and mash it with the other ingredients until thoroughly mixed. Use for sandwiches, toast or biscuits.

Family Chicken Sandwich

1 round loaf – granary or rye
  bread
3 lettuce leaves
2 tomatoes
30 ml (2 tablespoons) salad
  dressing
butter

Chicken Filling:
225 g (8 oz) cooked chicken
50 g (2 oz) Cheddar cheese
2 sticks celery
1 small green pepper
30 ml (2 tablespoons)
  mayonnaise

Egg Filling:
3 hard-boiled eggs
3 pickled gherkins
3 spring onions
30 ml (2 tablespoons)
  mayonnaise
1.2 ml ($\frac{1}{4}$ teaspoon) salt
dash of Tabasco sauce

Make the chicken filling first, by dicing the chicken finely, grating the cheese and chopping the celery and pepper to mix with the mayonnaise. Make the egg filling by chopping the eggs, gherkins and spring onions and mixing them with the mayonnaise and seasonings. Flavour and consistency are improved if this is done in advance and the fillings wrapped in foil and kept in the refrigerator for a few hours. Slice the loaf horizontally into four. Butter the bottom slice and spread this with egg filling – dribble a little salad dressing over this. Butter the next slice and place it on top. Arrange lettuce leaves and tomato slices on this and sprinkle with the dressing. Butter the next slice and place it on top with the dressing. Butter the next slice and place it on top. Spread it with the chicken filling and dribble dressing over it. Top this with the final slice and pierce six or eight cocktail sticks down through the loaf with (one for each serving) to hold the loaf together when cutting. To serve, cut downwards through the loaf into wedges. Eat with a knife and fork.

153

13　Freezing Poultry

A very high proportion of poultry is now bought frozen, either whole birds, joints, or ready-prepared dishes. It is also possible to freeze home-reared chickens and turkeys, and home-cooked poultry dishes may be frozen.

PREPARING BIRDS FOR THE FREEZER

Chicken and turkey are prepared in the same way for home-freezing, and may be packed whole or in portions. A bird should be in perfect condition and should be starved for 24 hours before killing, then hung and bled well. The bird should be plucked carefully, avoiding skin damage. If a bird is scalded to aid plucking, beware of over-scalding which increases the chance of freezer-burn (grey spots occurring during storage). The bird should be cooled in a refrigerator or cold larder for 12 hours, then drawn and completely cleaned. A whole bird should be neatly trussed to make a good shape for packing in the freezer.

Birds may be jointed for freezing, and either a whole bird may be packed together, or special bags made up of breasts, wings, drumsticks, etc. When home-packing poultry joints, pad the ends of the bones with small pieces of paper or foil to prevent any tears in the freezer wrapping. If you are likely to need only one or two joints at a time, wrap each one in freezer film before packing them in polythene bags. The high-quality storage life of whole birds is 8 months, and of portions 6 months.

GIBLETS

Do not pack the giblets inside the bird as they have a shorter storage life. This does not affect commercially packed birds which are quick-frozen and stored at very low temperatures. For home use, clean, wash, dry and chill the giblets, and pack them into polythene bags, excluding air. The high-quality storage life will be 2 months.

LIVERS

Poultry livers may be packed with other giblets, but they are so useful on their own that it is worth packing them separately. The high-quality storage life will be 2 months.

154

STUFFING

A bird should not be stuffed before freezing, as the storage life of stuffing is so short. Stuffing may be prepared, packed and frozen separately, although there is little advantage in this as it may easily be made separately while the bird is thawing. The high-quality storage life will be 1 month.

COOKED DISHES

Cooked casseroles and pies will freeze well and the high-quality storage life is 2 months. Roast and fried poultry frozen to be eaten cold, is not worth preparing as it takes a long time to thaw and will exude moisture and be flabby in texture when served. Slices of cold poultry can be frozen if divided by pieces of freezer film and packed tightly into a rigid box; or preferably they may be frozen in sauce which prevents them from drying out. Pâté and poultry loaves will freeze satisfactorily, with a high-quality storage life of 2 months. Stock made from poultry carcases can be boiled down to reduce the quantity and will keep for 2 months (stock can of course also be made into soup for freezing).

THAWING

Frozen poultry must be completely thawed before cooking. To obtain the best results, birds should be thawed slowly. They may be thawed in a refrigerator – presumed temperature 4.4°C (40°F) – or in a warm kitchen – presumed temperature 16°C (65°F). A useful table of thawing times is given on p 10.

Glossary

There are a few culinary terms which are particularly used in association with poultry, and which require some explanation for the amateur cook.

Bard   To cover breasts of poultry with thin slices of bacon or fat. Usually this is tied over the surface of the meat and melts during cooking, protecting the delicate breast meat and preventing it from becoming dry.

Baste   To drip fat or liquid, which has run out of food during cooking, over the food again to prevent a hardening of the skin or outer surface. This also helps to produce a golden finish for the food.

Boiling fowl   Old bird, usually a worn-out laying hen, which is suitable for cooking to make a variety of dishes and plenty of stock. These old birds are usually rather larger than today's oven-ready bird and will yield many meals, but take 3–4 hours to cook.

Breastbone   The end of the breastbone is a useful indication of age, as it becomes less supple in older birds.

Broil   To cook directly over a fire, or to grill (the word is used in America to describe our grilling process). In the early days of intensive chicken farming, battery chickens were referred to as 'broilers', reared in 'broiler houses'.

Capon   A male chicken which has been castrated when young to improve weight and flavour. These birds grow larger than cockerels and have well rounded bodies weighing 3–4 kg (6–8 lb).

Casserole   To cook in a covered earthenware, ovenglass or iron dish in the oven.

Crop   The pouch through which food passes before reaching the gizzard or food sac of the bird.

Devil   Dish made by coating cold leftover poultry with a very spicy thick sauce and grilling.

Drawing   Removing the internal organs and surplus fat from the inside of the bird.

Dressing   Plucking, singeing and cleaning birds before they are trussed, ie, tied for cooking.

156

Drumstick   The lower joint of a bird's leg.

Giblets   The liver, heart, gizzard and neck of the bird, usually packed inside the carcase when sold. In some countries, the pinions, feet, combs and kidneys are also included.

Lard   To pass small strips of fat through a bird with the aid of a special needle, to give richness to lean meat.

Marinade (Marinate)   To leave food to soak in a blend of wine, vinegar, spices and herbs to enrich flavour and soften flesh before cooking.

Pinion   The section of the wing beyond the outside joint.

Plucking   Removing feathers from a bird.

Poach   To cook gently in hot liquid just below boiling point, so that the shape of the food is retained.

Poussin   A baby chicken for one or two people.

Singeing   Removing the fine feathers and stumps of feathers over the flame of a candle or gas burner after plucking.

Stock   Liquid in which poultry has been cooked with vegetables, which can be used for soups, sauces and casseroles.

Trussing   Fixing the wings and legs of a bird to the body with skewers and string to make it into a neat shape which is attractive for cooking.

Index

158

159